Praise for

THE ZERO TRANSACTION COST ENTREPRENEUR

The late Oliver Williamson won the Nobel Prize in Economics for his pioneering work on transaction costs. Berkery's book brings this powerful perspective to entrepreneurs and explains how they can use transaction cost analysis to discover new entrepreneurial opportunities. The book is rich with compelling examples drawn from everyday life and successful startups. It will change the way that founders build new ventures.

—Thomas Eisenmann
professor at Harvard Business School

Forget the endless brainstorms, white boards, and business canvases. Use this book to uncover big new entrepreneurial ideas through its far more enjoyable and repeatable frameworks. If you've ever thought "this business/service/product would be so much better if . . ." then you've already started using the framework. *The Zero Transaction Cost Entrepreneur* dissects and supercharges those skills of observation and analysis to a powerful level, applicable to any business or industry.

—Jules Pieri
Cofounder of online marketplace The Grommet,
Harvard Business School Entrepreneur in Residence emeritus,
and author of *How We Make Stuff Now*

There is opportunity for innovation everywhere; the challenge is to identify compelling ideas before everyone else. The *Zero Transaction Cost Entrepreneur* lays out the novel theory that the key to spotting new opportunities first is to focus on eliminating transaction costs. In this engaging book, Dermot Berkery identifies different types of transaction costs and shows how, as they fall, opportunities to create businesses and industries proliferate.

—Tim Calkins
Clinical Professor of Marketing, Kellogg School
of Management, Northwestern University

At last! Creative genius for those of us that are rational. In *The Zero Transaction Cost Entrepreneur*, Berkery provides a handbook for jumpstarting entrepreneurship, from seeing unmet needs to structuring an organization to capture them. With a conversational, practical approach, he takes the mystery out of the process of finding great new business ideas.

—Elane Stock
former CEO at ServiceMaster Brands, previously
partner at McKinsey & Company

THE ZERO
TRANSACTION
COST
ENTREPRENEUR

THE ZERO TRANSACTION COST ENTREPRENEUR

POWERFUL TECHNIQUES TO REDUCE FRICTION AND SCALE YOUR BUSINESS

DERMOT BERKERY

New York Chicago San Francisco Athens London Madrid
Mexico City Milan New Delhi Singapore Sydney Toronto

1 2 3 4 5 6 7 8 9   LCR   28 27 26 25 24 23

ISBN   978-1-265-39991-7
MHID   1-265-39991-3

e-ISBN   978-1-265-40448-2
e-MHID   1-265-40448-8

Library of Congress Cataloging-in-Publication Data

Names: Berkery, Dermot, author.
Title: The zero transaction cost entrepreneur : powerful techniques to reduce
    friction and scale your business / by Dermot Berkery.
Description: New York : McGraw-Hill Education, [2024] | Includes
    bibliographical references and index. | Summary: "Harness the power of
    "zero transaction costs" to ensure long-term success in every new business
    proposition"— Provided by publisher.
Identifiers: LCCN 2023007016 (print) | LCCN 2023007017 (ebook) |
    ISBN 9781265399917 (hardback) | ISBN 9781265404482 (ebook)
Subjects: LCSH: New business enterprises. | Transaction costs.
Classification: LCC HD62.5 .B477 2024 (print) | LCC HD62.5 (ebook) |
    DDC 658.1/1—dc23/eng/20230605
LC record available at https://lccn.loc.gov/2023007016
LC ebook record available at https://lccn.loc.gov/2023007017

McGraw Hill books are available at special quantity discounts to use as premiums and sales promotions or for use in corporate training programs. To contact a representative, please visit the Contact Us pages at www.mhprofessional.com.

McGraw Hill is committed to making our products accessible to all learners. To learn more about the available support and accommodations we offer, please contact us at accessibility@mheducation.com. We also participate in the Access Text Network (www.accesstext.org), and ATN members may submit requests through ATN.

CONTENTS

PREFACE

12 Techniques for Generating
Great New Business Propositions

D o you want to become an entrepreneur, or are you a manager in a company that wants to generate new business propositions? Every company, tiny or large, should be thinking about future engines for growth. What are the business propositions that will drive fast growth in revenues in 5 to 10 years, beyond the proposition(s) that the company delivers to the market today? Every business proposition eventually becomes tired or is overcome by better competitors. Constant renewal is critical.

Yet business leaders struggle to identify these future engines for growth—they are often exclusively focused on near-term performance improvement. To the extent that long-term growth is on the strategic planning agenda of the company, it relates to growth within business units rather than the creation of new business units to add to and ultimately replace existing business units.

To build these future engines for growth, the first place to start is with great ideas for propositions that will excite customers (consumers and businesses) in future years. Too often, business leaders expect these ideas to bubble up from within the organization. Business leaders have the macro perspective on the market in which the company operates; they need to take back the process of idea generation. However, they need tools to do this; for too long, idea generation has been considered a creative process less suited to the analytically minded that populate the ranks of senior business leaders.

This book will help business leaders to take control of the process of idea generation. They will find 12 powerful techniques for generating new business propositions. These techniques leverage economic theory to provide insights to how the world will change in ways that might yield value to entrepreneurs and their customers. These techniques can applied to any sector in any location.

o o o

By the time you finish this book, you will be an idea generation machine for any sector to which you decide to turn your mind. Over to you to figure out which of your ideas might be world-beaters!

ACKNOWLEDGMENTS

The genesis of this book came from a course that I taught to graduate business students at University College Dublin. The course was titled the Economics of Entrepreneurship. In scratching my head regarding the creation of compelling content for the course, I ran headfirst into the big questions of this book. Where do ideas for new businesses come from? What is it that changes in the world that opens up opportunities for business propositions that weren't previously possible?

Then I stumbled into the world of shifting transaction costs. Although the foundational thinking on transaction costs goes back to Ronald Coase in 1937, the field is still fluid, and, more excitingly, I found that transaction costs have an all-powerful impact on new entrepreneurial propositions (and everything else in the world).

A lot of people gave me great (and some very robust!) feedback on the book content as it evolved, and the final shape of it owes a lot to that input. Many thanks to David Thompson, Alec Hudnut, Mike Marasco, Elizabeth Reynolds, Orla Byrne, Reed Benet, James Muldowney, Vernon Lobo, Stever Robbins, and others who volunteered to read it for me—the bruises are nearly healed.

Special thanks to my current and former colleagues in Delta Partners venture capital, with whom I have had 20-plus enjoyable years debating the merits and demerits of thousands of new business propositions.

Judith Newlin and the team at McGraw Hill spotted the potential in the book and were quick to encourage me to finish it and have been incredibly supportive in bringing it to market.

Finally, thanks to my family—Sally, Cormac, Rory, and Kathleen—who have finally figured out what dad was up to in his office until late at night.

THE ZER0 TRANSACTI0N C0ST ENTREPRENEUR

CHAPTER 1

Why Do Other People Come Up with All the Brilliant Ideas?

The popular press is full of stories of swashbuckling entrepreneurs dancing on the graves of staid old industries and, with a bit of magic, conjuring up billion-dollar businesses. These entrepreneurs are portrayed as creatively destructive geniuses who would put a smile on the face of Joseph Schumpeter. They seem larger than life with pearls of wisdom (all in hindsight, mind you) regarding how they foresaw the world about to turn on its axis and how they applied the coup de grâce to make it happen. The cult of personality surrounding these winners puts them on a pedestal like modern-day prophets—we expect them to show up at Davos and hand down tablets engraved with nuggets of wisdom about technology for poverty alleviation in war-torn nations or new techniques for saving the planet by boosting the libido of the humble bee.

What chance is there for the rest of us mere mortals who have never had an original thought? We seem to be lacking the great aha moments of these legendary entrepreneurs in their air-conditioned garages. We don't have billion-dollar ideas, never mind hundred-dollar ideas, even after we emerge from our annual weekend mindfulness retreat.

Yet, when we look at these brilliant ideas that our feted heroes came up with, we are bothered by the distinct (and deflating) feeling that "I could have thought of that." Think of the businesses that have grown from zero to huge valuations in recent years:

- **Tesla:** Hang on, weren't electric cars being discussed a hundred years ago?
- **Airbnb:** Started by helping people to couch surf, it now facilitates renting of apartments in Barcelona. Hadn't I booked many holiday rentals over the years by phone or even online, long before Airbnb?
- **Uber:** Haven't taxis and private car hire been around for a long time?

These are great businesses with remarkable valuations, but clearly their propositions are not rocket science or as challenging as curing cancer. So why did these entrepreneurs succeed?

One thing these entrepreneurs did well was to take these good ideas by the scruff of the neck and make them happen, execute them better than anyone else, normally earlier than everyone else (but not necessarily). Fair dues to them: who among us hasn't benefited by staying in a relatively inexpensive, Ikea-furnished apartment in Barcelona, owned by a charming lady named Carmen who is delighted to introduce us to her city and tell us where to get the best paella?

It is easy and churlish for the rest of us to look back and to say that those successful ideas were nothing magic. Everything is so clear in hindsight.

But the success of these entrepreneurs was about more than just trying hard. Their timing was perfect—the world truly was ready to turn on its axis. They were there to nudge it on its way.

The goal of this book is to help you to spot where the world is about to turn on its axis and to get your timing just right. It aims to help you to look forward and to develop an informed judgment regarding where you might capture value if you are inclined toward entrepreneurship. Crudely put, where are the fruitful places, right now and in the near future, where you might make lots of money?

o o o

So, where do we start? If you are an aspiring entrepreneur or a manager in a large company who wants to create a new business, the place to start is to generate revolutionary new business ideas. This book will help you to do so. Specifically, it is about turning you into an idea creation machine. Not by mind-bending brainstorming, but by the application of economics.

THE ANSWER IS IN THE ECONOMICS— TRANSACTION COST ECONOMICS

Transaction cost (TxC) economics are like physics. Physics determine how everything in the world behaves in relation to other things. TxC economics determine how everything should be *organized* in relation to every other thing.

While you are probably unfamiliar with transaction costs, hold this thought: *the way the world is organized today is due to the current landscape of TxCs.* Look around your home: how you live, everything you have, the way your home is constructed and laid out, where everything is located in your house, perhaps even the shape of your family—all are determined by TxCs. For example, items like your coffee maker, your toaster, and your kettle are probably sitting on your kitchen counter rather than in a cupboard. Why? Because you don't want to waste the time every day getting them in and out of a cupboard—the opportunity cost of your time (an important TxC) is too high. Look at the company you work for: the way that it is set up, the organizational structure, the processes it follows, whether it outsources a lot or not, its physical locations—these are all governed by the TxCs to which it is subject. Soon, you will be seeing TxCs everywhere.

Follow the analogy to the rules of physics: if we could relax a rule in physics, the way in which every object behaves and the way in which it relates to every other object would change. For example, if we could change the mathematical equation governing gravity, things would start flying around. Similarly, when TxCs fall (and fall they must, as you will soon discover), the way the world is organized starts to change—sometimes very rapidly, sometimes slowly or even imperceptibly. But, eventually, change it does; the fundamental economics always win.

Revolutionary new business ideas are based on the gap between (A) how things are organized today and (B) how they should be organized tomorrow. The difference between (A) and (B) is an opportunity for an entrepreneur. While you might not yet be ready to accept the proposition, I hope that within a short number of pages you will appreciate that the difference between (A) and (B) is solely due to TxCs falling.

○ ○ ○

What does this mean for entrepreneurship? *Entrepreneurship is the capture of value from falling TxCs.*

New business opportunities arise when TxCs fall as the world then becomes overdue a realignment in business activity and organization. If entrepreneurs (including ambitious managers in large companies and people in their garages, etc.) understand the changing landscape of TxCs, they will be well-placed to understand the value pools that are ripe to be tapped.

What is so exciting for entrepreneurs is that TxCs are falling. Indeed, many TxCs have been collapsing in recent decades and will collapse much further. Yet entrepreneurs have barely scraped the surface in taking advantage of this phenomenon. In general, the pace of decline over the millennia of human existence has been imperceptibly slow. Now, things are different; the TxCs are falling fast. As a result, the way the world is organized is a lot different from how the TxCs suggest it should be organized—there is a big gap between (A) and (B). It is as if the rules of physics have changed but the objects in the world have not yet realigned themselves to reflect the new rules. There is a glut of value in underexploited TxCs waiting to be unlocked by entrepreneurs.

We can't all be as creative as Steve Jobs—and we don't need to be. There are endless opportunities lying around waiting to be acted upon; we just need to put on the right set of glasses to find them—TxC glasses.

So, what exactly are TxCs in practice?

CHAPTER 2

Falling Transaction Costs: Blockbuster Versus Netflix

P erhaps the best way to bring TxCs to life is through a simple, well-known example. For those of us old enough to remember, Blockbuster video rental (and other similar rental companies) was fantastic. Beginning in 1985, those of us with kids could guarantee that we had a good movie to keep the crew entertained on a Saturday evening. No more hunting around to exchange armfuls of VHS tapes and (later) DVDs with friends and relatives or having a fruitless Saturday night hoping something decent showed up on TV. The latest, greatest movies showed up in Blockbuster not too long after general release in cinemas, and we all hurried down to the store to be first to get them. With babysitting at $8 to $10 an hour, a trip to the movie theater was an overpriced night out. Blockbuster's revenues grew into billions, and the distinctive blue movie ticket logo started to show up on main streets around the world. It is hard now to remember how good we all thought it was at the time.

After movies began to be available on DVD in 1997, in 1998 Netflix introduced its DVD-by-mail service. Customers paid a monthly fee and created a queue of movies that they wanted to see. The faster they watched them and returned them by mail, the more movies they got to see. The service was reasonably successful, and even as of 2021 had revenues of $182 million.*

---

* Netflix Financial Statements, Q3, 2022.

In 2007 Netflix again embraced new technology and launched its online video streaming service, and in a very short period streaming wiped the floor with the earlier video delivery methods; the main street rental store went the way of the dinosaurs. In hindsight it was obvious—streaming is clearly immensely more appealing to consumers; try explaining the concept of video rental stores to people under the age of 25.

Yet, at the time, it wasn't so obvious as we feel it is now. People loved Blockbuster (other than those bothersome late-return fees). Indeed, Blockbuster could have pursued its own streaming service but declined to commit to it.

As we look back, the Saturday escapade becomes a bit clearer. It involved a minor negotiation with my spouse about who was going to go and get the DVD, a drive with the kids to the rental store with a hassle to find parking, and firm instructions to get a light rom-com when I was aiming to get a culturally enhancing action movie starring Arnold Schwarzenegger, and the kids wanted something with happy music and dancing penguins. Of course, unless I got there early on the Saturday, all the newly released movies were long gone (for which they wanted to charge you two or three times the normal movie price anyway). After lots of disputes, we all had to sit down at the same time to watch it. Worst of all, we had to endure the drive to the rental store for drop-off (after another marital discussion), often missing the deadline by five minutes and having to pay a late fee. Looking back, it was almost comedic, but at the time we all flocked to use it.

o o o

All those hassles with getting a DVD from Blockbuster were transaction costs. In the words of economists, TxCs are inhibitors to exchange—they either prevent us from consuming what we would like to consume, or they reduce the rate at which we consume. We would like to watch a certain movie, but we must jump through all sorts of hoops to see it. In fact, we never wanted a DVD; we wanted to be entertained by immersing ourselves in a great visual story. This is an important distinction that we will return to throughout this book.

When the TxCs come down and there are fewer inhibitors to exchange, people consume in new ways; they also can increase their rate of consumption in unforeseen new ways. "Aha!" the numerically inclined people will say—Blockbuster cost about $5 for a good movie, and we can watch many hours of video on Netflix for roughly $10 to $20 a month. The financial cost per hour of video is much less—so why wouldn't people consume more? This is just simple supply and demand curves.

But clearly the reduced financial cost is not the true reason people are watching a lot of video—the financial cost is irrelevant to the discussion. The real TxCs with Blockbuster were those of getting and returning the DVD, the marital discussions, the limited selection, the empty shelves, the late fees, and the general hassles. These TxCs placed boundaries on the lives of consumers around the world. Consumers wanted a certain movie at a certain time (often right now), and someone had placed an obstacle course in front of them to prevent them from getting it.

As a test of the power of reduced TxCs (one TxC is the opportunity cost of my time, which we will explore later), subscribers to Netflix were apparently watching an average of 3.2 hours per day in the middle of the Covid-19 pandemic.[*] Compare this to a 1.5 hour per week movie from Blockbuster. We cannot even begin to count the hours spent watching other videos on various social networks, how-to videos on the internet when an appliance breaks down, dancing cats on YouTube, and so on.

o o o

Transaction costs (TxCs) are those costs incurred in an exchange between two parties that are not to the benefit of either party. Party A and party B want to do business with each other, but TxCs get in the way—they are the friction that inhibits or prevents the exchange. TxCs may sound complicated and best suited to a technical conversation between mathematically adept economists. But nothing could be further from the truth. They are, instead, the hidden strings that shape and govern our lives.

---

[*] Jason Cohen, "U.S. Netflix Subscribers Watch 3.2 Hours and Use 9.6 GB of Data Per Day," *PCMag*, May 2020, https://www.pcmag.com/news/us-netflix-subscribers-watch-32-hours-and-use-96-gb-of-data-per-day.

CHAPTER 3

Falling Transaction Costs Will Lead to Perfection in Our Lives

D ue to video streaming, we have incredible quantities of video to consume at our fingertips. Want to watch every season of *Breaking Bad* or *The Sopranos*? No problem. Interested in the endless cooking programs by every chef under the sun? No problem. Want to share a funny video on Facebook of a cat talking? No problem. Need to see the goals from last night's football game that you missed? No problem. The entirety of films, TV series, and other video filmed in the world is almost at our fingertips, and we think nothing of it.

On the video-watching front, we can glimpse the future— our lives will become progressively perfect. For our purposes perfection means *we have whatever we want, whenever we want it, and it will be simple to access.*

That's where we are headed; perfection is a world of zero transaction costs. TxCs are the hassles that we must endure while trying to get our wants and needs met. But TxCs are on a one-way journey in the general direction of zero—not that zero on every TxC dimension is ever really achievable, except perhaps in infinite years. Zero TxCs would mean that we could click our fingers (or have a thought) and every single need or want would be fulfilled instantly, to perfection. It sounds ridiculous; clearly this is all a very long way away in many areas of our lives.

PERFECTION IS COMING QUICKLY IN DIGITIZABLE ASPECTS OF PEOPLE'S LIVES

Along every dimension of people's lives, TxCs are falling—some rapidly, and some very slowly. The fall in TxCs is relaxing the constraints on people's lives, sometimes even constraints of which they were and are completely unaware. Lower constraints open up possible new business models. The reduction in TxCs in the Netflix example demonstrates one way the constraints on consumption can be lifted.

People will find that perfection may come quickly in areas of life that can be digitized. We have a taste for what perfection might mean in these areas, and we like it a lot. When our wants are met perfectly by a service, the way we consume that service becomes more intense. We can type a query into a search engine and get an answer to almost any question a human can pose. Many books are already digitized and available at any time and any place. We have access to ubiquitous video. We think nothing of the ability to phone a large percentage of the world's population and talk to them instantaneously (and often for free or for zero marginal cost to the provider). We are irritated if we leave our phone at home and lose our "always on" capability. Our relationship with social media is often described as addictive.

We are well on our way to perfection in these areas. Or at least, that is how it looks from the vantage point of today; maybe in a few years the video-watching world will be a Netflix-type service, or maybe it won't. Maybe the service we are getting from Netflix and the other streaming services today will go the way of the Blockbusters of yesteryear. Perhaps the Netflix of today will be looked on as just another intermediary whose goal was to get between consumers and the movie producers and extract their monthly fee (a portion of which they pass back to the video creators). Maybe soon TxCs will be low enough for us not to need Netflix, as we as consumers will be contracting one-by-one directly with the movie producers to have them produce what we want. Maybe then the movie producer will then just be another intermediary that is getting between us and the true talent—the wonderful actors, directors, and screenwriters.

Maybe TxCs will fall low enough to allow me as a consumer to contract directly with George Clooney and Steven Spielberg for my specific wants. Maybe in the year 2040 we will look back on these supposed areas of perfection and laugh at how primitive and high TxC our consumption of video, books, and music was in 2023. How fascinating such a world would be!

Our world will be continuously reshaped as falling TxCs open exciting business model possibilities.

IN MANY SECTORS, PERFECTION SEEMS TO BE A LONG WAY AWAY

Other than digitizable products and services, we have many other wants where things are a long way away from being *perfect*. Indeed, the notion of perfection is inconceivable to us for mundane wants like personal services (hair styling, physiotherapy), trades (plumbing, electrics, construction), or last mile delivery. For these wants, we get more of a high-TxC Blockbuster-type experience than a Netflix one. With these nondigitizable wants, we are plagued with TxCs such as an inability to search the market, problems trusting suppliers, and the tyranny of geography (more on these in later chapters). But, as we will see, even these knotty TxCs continue to be eroded, and new ways of meeting customers' mundane wants and needs will become possible, in the manner that video streaming wiped out DVDs. Perfection is where we are headed, and not just for wants that can be served digitally.

THE ROLE OF THE ENTREPRENEUR

This is where the role of the entrepreneur comes in: *entrepreneurship is the capture of value from falling TxCs.*

The exciting part of being an entrepreneur is trying to figure out what happens next. Where are the places where value will be available to be captured on the TxC journey? Which TxC has fallen, but other entrepreneurs have yet to take advantage?

Which TxCs will fall next that the entrepreneur should position herself against before anyone else?

While perfection is the destination, what is most important to entrepreneurs is the journey. The entrepreneur needs to take advantage of the difference between the landscape of TxCs today and TxCs tomorrow. Falling TxCs signpost the pathway to perfection by progressively unlocking the possibility of new business models. Lower TxCs allow customer needs to be met in new ways.

○ ○ ○

Of the 12 techniques for generating revolutionary new business ideas using TxC thinking that we will explore in this book, the first is that of *imagining perfection.*

TECHNIQUE A:
IMAGINING PERFECTION

PERFECT FULFILLMENT OF OUR WANTS

A great place to start hunting for exciting new business propositions and new products is to explore what it would take for the consumer or business customer's underlying want to be met *perfectly*. Perfectly means a zero TxC satisfaction of my wants and needs, but *perfectly* is a more powerful and simpler concept for us to conceive of—a lot easier than asking people to imagine "a zero TxC experience."

Ultimate perfection in the eyes of the customer might be a proposition that would be impossible for any entrepreneur to deliver, except perhaps in some very distant future scenario. But if we know what perfection looks like, we have a chance of reconceiving the existing product or service and generating a new entrepreneurial proposition that begins to take the customer in the right direction on the perfection journey.

For example, let's start with buying an ice cream from an ice cream shop. This activity is about as simple as it gets. How could the fulfillment of that want (occasionally a need!) be made perfect?

TxCS IN THE ICE CREAM EXPERIENCE

Tucking into an ice cream on a sunny afternoon is already pretty high up on the list of life's wonderful experiences. What might possibly be done to make it a perfect experience? Thankfully, most of us (author included) are unencumbered by knowledge of the business of ice cream (other than as consumers), so we can be liberal with our ideas.

So why isn't the ice cream experience completely perfect? Let's start with a few concerns, in no particular order:

- Why does ice cream melt faster than I can consume it?
- Why do I need to handle it carefully to avoid it dripping and ending up on my jeans?

- Why is my cone given to me at a temperature not quite cold enough to last until I manage to lick it down? Or as the economists might say: Why does the melt rate exceed the normalized lick rate? I suspect this is due to the need to make it scoopable for the server—but that should be their problem, not mine.
- Why does ice cream contain so many things that are bad for me (sugar, fat, etc.)? Yet these are probably the things that lead me to pine for the product in the first place.
- Why on earth do they serve ice cream for small kids on the same precariously balanced cones as everyone else's? We all know these are going to end up on the ground and induce temper tantrums.
- Why do I experience embarrassment when I get to the front of the line and start to get interrogated by the server as to which flavor I want, which toppings, which cone or cup or sundae? Why does it feel like I need a master's degree in ice cream design?
- How do you really expect me to order flavors such as Pralines 'N Cream, Daiquiri Ice, and Rainbow Sherbet when I have no idea what they might taste like?
- Why can't I have an ice cream in my hand right when I want it? Now that I am writing about ice cream and my taste buds are tingling, why can't I have one in my hand right now?
- Why do I need to drive roughly two miles to the nearest decent ice cream shop?
- Why do I end up with an ice cream in my hands fewer times than I actually want one?
- Why are the lines always ridiculously long right when I want my ice cream? Surprisingly, we all seem to want them at the same time—midafternoon on a lovely day!
- Why is the making of an ice cream and fulfillment of the order so slow? How many times have I abandoned my quest mid-queue after realizing that there is a parent with a gaggle of indecisive kids between me and my ice cream?
- Why do servers sometimes touch cones with bare hands? Why do they have to handle dirty cash as well?

- Why do I have to eat it in the car or hustle to find a public bench to eat it on?
- Why can't I have the perfect ice cream store quality experience at home (given that the treats will be half-melted and messy by the time I drive home)?
- Why can't I hold the cone and drive?
- Why isn't ice cream available 24/7?
- Why is the experience of an ice cream from an ice cream shop so much better than tucking into a tub from the freezer?
- Why is the price I am charged always much more than I expected it would be when I showed up at the shop?

DISTILLING THE MOST PRESSING TxC TO CREATE THE PERFECT ICE CREAM

While there are a bunch of "imperfections" to the ice cream experience, the most powerful TxCs seem to be those that inhibit me from getting my hands on an ice cream cone right when I want one. The shop is too far away, the lines are too long, the process takes too long, the effort to get the ice cream in my hand is too much. If I were to hazard a guess, it is possible that the ratio of times that I would like an ice cream in my hand compared to the times that I end up having one in my hand is probably 20 to 1 or maybe even 50 to 1. While I might be sitting on my couch an hour after dinner and pining after an ice cream, the pain of getting up from my comfy seat and driving to get one is way too high. Pity the ice cream entrepreneur—she is getting a tiny fraction of the business that she should be getting from me.

In summary, we have vast numbers of thwarted ice cream exchanges—perhaps only 2 to 5 percent of the possible exchanges end up taking place. The TxCs of getting an ice cream in my hand right when I want it are, on examination, incredibly and surprisingly high. While I might not increase my consumption rate 20 times or 50 times due to my desire to avoid a midlife coronary, if the ice cream could be made more on-demand for me in some way, the amount of exchange could surely be multiplied.

It turns out that the perfect ice cream is not the one with the fanciest flavor; it is the rare one that shows up in my fist right when the pangs of desire are crying out.

HOW TO REDUCE THE TxC

So how might we make the ice cream process a bit more on-demand than it is today? We are a long way from me being able to click my fingers and have a delicious cone in my hand right here and now. Yes, I could break open a tub at home, but it is not as fulfilling an experience. Surely there must be a way to unpack the TxCs that cause more than 95 percent of my potential exchanges with the ice cream shop to be thwarted.

Here is where we need to defer to our budding entrepreneur who sets out to disrupt the ice cream world. Yes, he or she could set up a streamlined ice cream shop with faster service and easier choices. But the real opportunity for bringing a radical new proposition to the market seems to be in reducing the time and barriers from ice cream impulse to ice cream in hand. Perhaps the entrepreneur needs to do some research on the half-life of a person's ice cream desire—how many minutes of high desire does the entrepreneur have to get an ice cream in my hand before the craving abates?

With this knowledge, maybe the entrepreneur could think about:

- As delivery-to-the-home (last mile) services improve, could ice cream packaging be redesigned to fit into such a delivery system?
- Could a Nespresso-type machine be developed for in-home use that delivers ice cream shop quality ice cream to the consumer in the kitchen with ready-to-use sachets? This sounds really good!
- Should we bring back the ice cream trucks of our youth that patrolled the neighborhoods and subdivisions blaring Pavlovian jingles and sending rabid kids into their homes to torment their parents for a few dollars?

This was a wonderful, low-TxC, instant-gratification offering.
* Could the store-bought ice cream tubs be upgraded into an ice cream shop quality product?

Let's leave it up to the entrepreneurs to figure out the best answer. We know there is significant latent demand, exhibited by the very large number of unfulfilled exchanges—ice cream entrepreneurs have the chance to sell much more ice cream.

o o o

As our example shows, to be an ice cream entrepreneur, one does not need to think deeply and expertly about the physics and flavors of ice cream. But please invent an ice cream that doesn't melt nearly as quickly while still giving that sweet frozen experience!

Your job is an entrepreneur is to exploit decreasing TxCs and to crush or sidestep existing TxCs. During the process of imagining perfection, it is best to simply ignore costs. Better to start by positing what the most perfect satisfaction of the person's need would be. Besides, a typical $5 to $7 ice cream is full of fat, both digestively and financially.

CHAPTER 4

Falling Transaction Costs →
Increased Exchange →
Opportunities for Entrepreneurs
and Value for Everyone

I f the long-term implication of falling TxCs is perfection in our lives, what is the economic process by which the falling TxCs help entrepreneurs to realize value? *Value is created through exchange.*

The world generates more value over time, as shown by the improvement in the average quality of life over centuries and decades. As citizens of the world, we are the beneficiaries of this one-way gravy train that improves our lives. That is not to say that there are not bad periods due to natural disasters, war, or damaging governmental actions, or that value gets shared equitably across the population. But over the long term, things get better and we have more value in our lives. Not many of us would sign up to go back in time even to the so-called Golden Age of the 1950s. What is this relentless value creation machine that has been at work since the dawn of humankind? How do we spin straw into gold?

EXCHANGE IS HOW VALUE IS CREATED

Exchange is the mechanism through which the world creates *value*. For the non-economically minded, instead of value use the word *happiness*. It's pretty close to the same thing.

For the very economically minded, replace happiness with the word *utility*. Only the economists could have picked so nondescript a word for such a wonderful thing!

Value, *happiness*, and *utility*—they all connote the betterment of people's lives. I will use them interchangeably throughout the book, but I will primarily use *value*, as that will resonate most with the reader of this book—those of you interested in uncovering entrepreneurial opportunities.

HOW DOES VALUE GET CREATED THROUGH THE MEDIUM OF EXCHANGE?

If I decide to buy a painting for $100 from a street vendor, the two of us have created and captured value. The painting is worth less than $100 to her, or else she wouldn't be selling it for $100. The painting is worth more to me than $100, or I wouldn't have paid the price. Through that exchange, we have created more value in the world—more happiness for each, as neither of us would have engaged in the exchange unless it made each of us happier. In theory we could have bartered (exchanged) a few hours of my time as a finance professional for the time it took her to create the painting, but it is far easier to exchange through the mutually recognized medium of money. Prior to the creation of money, the lack of such a mutually recognized medium would have been a colossal TxC—I would not have been able to get a painting without finding someone who wanted my particular skills (or finding a circular group of people where we could all meet each other's needs simultaneously).

Exchange is the magic that delivers happiness and value in our lives. Every exchange creates value. More exchanges mean more value and more happiness, as each party enters the exchanges voluntarily with the goal of extracting value from them.

But exchanges are not just the cold-blooded back-and-forth trade inherent to the capitalistic world. Exchanges can be as simple as:

* Two neighbors agree that parent A will pick the kids up from school on Monday if parent B picks the kids up on Tuesday.
* Neighbor A lends a hammer to neighbor B. Neighbor A gets the pleasure of being considered a good fellow citizen; neighbor B saves a wasted hour going to the hardware store just to knock in a nail.
* Kid A swaps the apple in his lunch for one of kid B's cookies.

In each of these cases, people walk away happier and value has been created, even though it might not show up in the Gross Domestic Product quarterly figures.

Each of us is exchanging thousands of times, if not tens of thousands, every day, and we are completely unaware that we are doing it. When we stock up at the grocery store, we are exchanging with countless other parties. If I buy a chocolate bar, I am setting off an incredible cascade of exchange. Initially with the retailer, but from there to the chocolate bar company, the workers in the chocolate bar factory, the importer of the cocoa beans, the freight ship owner, the guy who transported the beans to the port, the cocoa bean grower in Guatemala, and so forth, almost endlessly and essentially unconsciously. I am exchanging when I have a tacit agreement with my spouse— "you put the kettle on, and I will make the tea." When I pick up a book, I am exchanging with the publisher and to some extent with the author. When I buy coffee, I am exchanging with the barista, the owner of the coffee shop, the bean grower, the coffee bean cooperative in Colombia. Every time we voluntarily interact with another person, we are exchanging; I am exchanging when I text my friends during the game about how useless the opposition team is.

All these micro-exchanges add value to our lives and the lives of our counterparties. The mind-boggling complexity of some exchanges is a testament to the ability of the market mechanism to mediate most of these exchanges and coordinate vast, complex supply chains. These are not frictionless supply chains, but over the years as the TxC gremlins get zapped out of the system, they get smoother and smoother, exchange is easier, and value goes up.

TRANSACTION COSTS ARE BAD AS THEY INHIBIT EXCHANGE

Things that would have prevented a valuable exchange are bad; that's what TxCs are. They are the sand that fouls up the gears of commerce by imposing costs on the exchange that don't accrue to the benefit of either party. They become tangible and intangible costs that need to be borne by the two parties to the exchange, just to make the exchange happen. Indeed, most of the time TxCs don't just make exchange difficult—they make it uneconomic or impossible.

TxCs are not obvious and often need a forensic-style examination to be unearthed and understood. Let's revert to my street vendor example: What if I only had a credit card and the street vendor couldn't take a card for payment? Maybe I don't regularly walk in the part of the city where she displays her work because that part of the city does not seem safe to me or is off the beaten path. What if she and I don't speak the same language? Perhaps I didn't know the painting was for sale. I could go on and on. There are endless possible TxCs that could get in the way of the value-creating exchange. In fact, it is almost a minor miracle that the exchange happens.

Most potentially valuable exchanges do not happen, due to TxCs. Recall the ice cream example from Chapter 3: I exchange with the ice cream store owner (and the maker of the ice creams, the farmer who produces the milk, etc.) perhaps only once in every 50 times that I get the craving for an ice cream.

FALLING TxCS MULTIPLY EXCHANGE, THEREBY CREATING VALUE

For entrepreneurs, every fall in a TxC is manna from heaven. A fall in a TxC means that exchanges that were previously blocked by that TxC are now possible. The fall kicks off the start of an entrepreneurial race to make those exchanges happen and to capture the pot of value that was previously impossible to capture.

What does "falling TxCs" mean in the case of our street vendor? Prior to the internet, I had an *inability to search the market* (a classic TxC). If I wanted a painting of the seashore with the sun shining, I had to walk the streets of Dublin on a Sunday afternoon with only a limited expectation that I would find such a painting. Maybe I would see something I liked; maybe I wouldn't. Either way, I had an extremely limited choice, and I probably walked away with the feeling that I had been offered suboptimal options. This made me unlikely to exchange, or if I did, likely to have a less valuable exchange experience.

Contrast that with today, following the advent of the internet. That TxC (*an inability to search the market*) is reduced. I can search Dublin, Cork, Galway, not to mention London and further afield. The full market is potentially at my fingertips, especially if an entrepreneur has done her homework and created a business that lists lots of artists and their work. The chances of finding something that matches my needs, and being content that I have successfully scoured the market are higher. Consequently, I am far more likely to undertake an exchange. An increased ability to search the market has created value in the market for art.

Another hypothetical example: Let's assume a new cargo train line is due to open between China and India in the coming years. Today, overland trade between the two countries is almost impossible due to the Himalayas sitting in the middle; consequently, the physical and financial TxCs of moving goods overland are overwhelming. Exchange is inhibited by the *tyranny of geography* (one of the most challenging TxCs to overcome). A new train line will slice away some of those TxCs. Savvy Indian and Chinese entrepreneurs will spot that, with the impending fall in TxCs, new corridors of trade (new forms of exchange) will arise that were not previously possible. Goods will flow from one country to the other like water flowing downhill. For example, if today a metric ton of wheat sells for $100 in India and $200 in China, and it costs $50 to move the wheat on the new train line, there will be happy entrepreneurs and consumers excited take advantage of this new opportunity to exchange.

o o o

In this chapter we've discussed how exchange is the process through which value is created. Transaction costs are what get in the way of exchange and prevent this value from being created. In Technique A, we explored how a more perfect (less TxC) ice cream offering might lead to a new business opportunity for ice cream entrepreneurs. In Technique B, we will explore how reducing TxCs might lead to consumers or businesses driving up the velocity of their consumption of a product or service.

TECHNIQUE B:
DRIVING UP THE VELOCITY OF CONSUMPTION

In technique A, we searched for new propositions by *imagining perfection* and used it to conceive new product and service offerings for consumers and businesses. We looked at a simple product (ice cream) and explored how a perfection mindset might lead to new ice cream propositions.

In technique B, we will not look for new products and services. Instead, we will hunt out sectors and products where smart entrepreneurs might get us to drive up the velocity of our consumption of existing products and services.

As a reminder: TxCs suppress consumption by getting in the way of exchange. They force us to consume less of the product or service than we might otherwise like. If the entrepreneur could reduce the TxCs, the critical question is—what happens? Does consumption:

* Stay the same? This indicates that the customers (consumer or business) are fully sated with the quantity of the product or service that they are currently consuming.
* Increase a bit?
* Increase a lot? If so, might that be the basis for creating a new entrepreneurial business model?

BINGE-WATCHING ON NETFLIX

Consumption of video is a good example of lower TxCs leading to higher velocity of consumption. When I had to go through all the hassles of getting a video from Blockbuster, my consumption was probably limited to, at most, one or two rented movies a week. I certainly wasn't sitting at home thinking how wonderful it would be if I could consume a lot more video. If asked at the time, I would probably have sniffed that the opportunity cost of my time was way too high for me to be wasting it watching video.

People are incredibly poor judges of how they will behave in the future. Roll forward in time, and now I am binge-watching on Netflix. Who would have projected that we would sit down at

10 p.m. for some low-TxC viewing on Netflix, planning on a quick episode of some show, only to peel ourselves from the couch five episodes later at 2 a.m. with deep regret regarding the impending alarm at 6:45 a.m.? The low TxCs of just clicking the "Next Episode" button made watching a cliff-hanging crime series irresistible. Furthermore, the Covid-19 pandemic's social distancing requirements reduced the opportunity cost of people's time (previously a limiting TxC factor), letting the velocity of video consumption rise even higher, closer to its "natural" no-TxC level.

PRESSING THE NESPRESSO BUTTON ONE MORE TIME

Coffee machines like Nespresso are a great example of a TxC-reduction innovation that drove up the velocity of consumption. They create the allure of a coffee, as if made by a barista, at your fingertips by simply popping in a pod and pressing a button. It's almost as simple as clicking your fingers. Push-button coffee machines are designed to stimulate higher velocity usage. There is the simple instant gratification of hearing the innards of the machine working up to deliver its elixir. A true on-demand, low-TxC moment—but not quite.

Pity that we need yet another device that clogs up our valuable, waist-high, close-to-hand kitchen countertop. Not to mention the endless, wasteful empty pods. The pods contain small amounts of ground beans and don't deliver up a regular (largish) cup of coffee. The coffee is not terribly hot. All-in-all, the machines are designed for repeated use, and all we need to do is to press a button. Who can resist a refill in the middle of that boring web video meeting?

COULD LOWER TxCS INCREASE THE VELOCITY OF MEN'S HAIRCUTS?

A man's haircut is probably one of the most mundane personal services in a man's life (for most men, anyway). It is a must-do chore that hasn't seen a lot of technology or business model change since the advent of the first barber many centuries ago, except perhaps better scissors. Does it make sense for a brave entrepreneur to redesign the haircut experience with the goal of driving up the velocity of male haircuts?

Let's raise the bar—what could the entrepreneur do that would motivate me to get my hair cut every single day? A ridiculous goal, perhaps, but if my fellow citizens are willing to absorb the opportunity cost of spending three hours a day watching Netflix, who knows.

So, how do things work today? I get my hair cut every six weeks or so, and judging by the statistically insignificant poll that I conducted among my male peers, I am close to the median. The general sentiment is "six weeks is the longest that I can get away with before the John, Paul, George, and Ringo jokes start coming out." The visit to the barber is often initiated by a prod from one's spouse or some facetious comment from a friend, followed inevitably after the haircut by the "you got your money's worth" retorts. It is never a regularly scheduled event. My barber doesn't send me reminder emails as my dentist kindly does. Need just creeps up on me, and then it is time to get it cut as soon as possible.

I trudge to the barber on foot or by car. A slow push to open the door, praying that the lines are not ridiculous.

Hooray! A few people, not too many; great—time to settle in to clear some email and read an old magazine or a newspaper while the line whittles down (why can't we book a time as women can?). Same haircut as always—"hairstyle" would be a very generous interpretation of what I get. Bit of chitchat. Pay in cash—it is normally decent value at $15 to $20 a cut. It's probably a 1.5- or 2-hour-plus process door-to-door from my house and back, but often it's worse. The main TxC is the opportunity cost of my time.

On a bad visit, I open the door and there is a long line of teenage boys looking for hair styling rather than a haircut, and elderly men for whom going to the barber is a social event. Then there is a choice. Do I roll my eyes, walk away, and think about coming back the following week, or do I settle in grumpily at the back of the long line? As a Monday-to-Friday worker, I can only get to the barber on Saturdays, right when everyone else just like me is there as well. Having to wait until another day is the worst outcome—more opportunity cost of my time burned up.

Contrary to what most men will admit, after the hair is cut, one has a good vibe regarding being tidy and fit to rejoin the human race after a few shaggy weeks. Exchanging a haircut with the barber is a value-adding event in my life, at least to some minor degree.

To entice me to get my hair cut every day, the entrepreneur would have to drive my TxCs down almost to zero—to make the haircut as minimal hassle as it possibly could be. Is this possible? Entrepreneurs have redesigned the shaving and bathing processes to make them a daily activity for a sizeable share of the male population. Why not haircuts?

So, is there an opportunity to drive up the velocity of haircuts? The first place to start is by understanding the demand curve that different segments of men face for haircuts (Figure 4.1). Specifically, given different levels of TxCs on the Y axis ranging from the current high levels to much lower levels, how many haircuts per month are different segments likely to opt for? Do all men experience the demand curve on the left where, no matter what the TxCs, they are just going to get their hair cut every month or so?

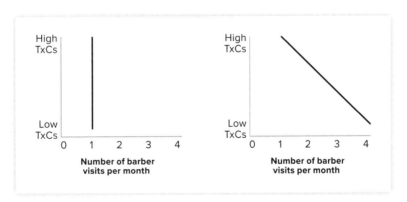

Figure 4.1 Two Demand Curves for Haircuts

Or is there a segment of men, illustrated by the graph on the right, where lowering the TxCs might coax them to increase their haircut velocity—maybe to twice a month? And if the hassles were to be reduced to a particularly low level (e.g., if the man had a barber permanently on call and metaphorically living in his spare bedroom, ready to be called on at short notice), might there be a small segment of men who would get happiness or utility from a haircut each week or even many times each week?

In summary, is there latent demand among certain segments of men for more frequent haircuts that is going unfulfilled? If so, which specific TxCs need to be relaxed or crushed to tap into this latent demand? It is the job of the entrepreneur to figure out if there is a cohort of men on the right side of the graph in Figure 4.1 who might, as the hassles go down, start getting their hair cut twice a month or even every week or on-demand as the mood strikes them.

How could those TxCs be lowered? By faster haircuts? Home or work visits? Online booking? Maybe a streaming camera that lets me see if there is a long line of people in front of me—are there kids or older people ahead of me for whom the opportunity cost of their time is a lot lower than mine?

Do the following segments exist for more frequent haircuts?

- **Segment one:** Men for whom the key issue is the opportunity cost of their time—they just can't get a haircut right at the time when they want one, and the end-to-end process takes way too long. They are too busy and their time is valuable. They might have a black-tie event this evening, in which case a fast haircut around 6 p.m. or a quick lunchtime cut when work is slow would be fantastic. For this segment, the opportunity cost of their time is a high multiple of the opportunity cost of a barber's time, so they may be willing to pay a very high price. The entrepreneur needs to figure out how to overcome the opportunity cost of the customer's time. Here's where we get into the realm of pure speculation: Maybe the entrepreneur could set up a swarm of roving barbers along the lines of a network of Uber drivers. Maybe barbers come to people's work location or home at set times or on-demand. Maybe the barber sets up a moveable kiosk like a food truck. Whatever the answer, the key requirement is one of reduced time for customers. The ultimate stretch goal for the entrepreneur is to collapse the end-to-end time for the consumer from, say, two hours to the 10 to 20 minutes required to cut the hair—no travel or wait time.

- **Segment two:** Men who are willing to sign up for a subscription service. Maybe this might appeal to men who like the idea of having a quick weekly trim (in off-peak hours for the barber).
- **Segment three:** Men for whom a haircut is a truly happy experience who might like a daily hair styling or professional blow-drying. In extremis, the stylist might come at a designated time each day for 10 minutes. The stylist then travels a few minutes for his or her next appointment, so that he or she can cut several heads of hair per hour. The customer pays for the service by subscription, and somehow or other the entrepreneur has turned it into a simple on-demand service that is not much more complicated for the customers than their daily shave or 10-minute shower.

Do these options make economic sense for the deliverer of this service and, consequently, for the customer? Probably not for most men who fall resolutely in the once-a-month haircut brigade. But without doing some research on the impact of the TxCs, it is difficult to know. Ten years ago, a roving barber service would have made no sense except for those willing to pay an incredibly high price. With the advent of GPS and the potential to create a swarm of barbers, the dead time between cutting heads of hair could be reduced to minutes, and such a barber would be able to avoid all the overhead of a main street location.

The point of this discussion is not to propose an impending Netflix-like revolution in the haircutting business. The hair-cutting business here is a proxy for all the relatively mundane products and services that we consume in our daily lives, without giving a flicker of thought to them. It is up to the smart entrepreneur to conceive and test reduced-TxC propositions that might drive up the velocity of usage and create new business models.

○ ○ ○

For example, here are two business models that exploit reduced TxCs to offer higher velocity hair care propositions:

Business Model 1: Quick Barber

Quick Barber in Japan offers 10-minute haircuts for about $8. They reengineered the process for cutting hair to make it faster and more environmentally friendly. There is a traffic light system outside the shop to tell customers the exact wait time. The shops are located in places like train stations, and people can tell how long they have until their train arrives and figure out if they have sufficient time for a haircut. The locations are not chosen as destinations, but rather as places where the consumer might happen to be, with dead time (which means low opportunity cost) on their hands.

One interesting question for Quick Barber: Do the reduced TxCs offered by Quick Barber increase the demand for haircuts, or does the consumer pocket the benefit of the reduced TxCs and still only get one haircut each month?

Business Model 2: Blow-Dry Bars

Blow-dry bars for women have experienced a boom in recent years. The words they use to describe themselves point to the desire for increased velocity of consumption given lower TxCs:

- "Any day of the week"
- "A little bit of everyday glamour"
- "Repertoire of styles"
- "For a fraction of the price"
- "40 minutes or less"
- "Lasts for three to five days"

○ ○ ○

The next chapter gives an overview of the eight major categories of TxCs. These will be explored individually in depth throughout the book.

CHAPTER 5

The Eight Major Categories of Transaction Costs

E veryone hates paying commissions, margins, fees, transaction fees, brokers' fees, introduction fees, and buy-sell spreads. We resent paying for what we see as nothing—nothing in this case just being the person who sits in the middle and takes a seemingly undeserved clipping out of our transactions. We tar real estate agents, stockbrokers, insurance brokers, and other introducers with the brush of being necessary evils. They exist to help make transactions happen by simplifying exchange for the customer and supplier; the downside is that they need to be paid.

These "bad" monetary TxCs get all the attention. Discussions of monetary TxCs rapidly end up in a cul-de-sac view of the future in which all intermediaries (middlemen) will eventually be wiped out by the internet—and good riddance to them. This wiping out of today's intermediaries may happen, but new models of inter-mediation are likely to come to the fore in the short-to-medium term. For example, ride-sharing companies or online marketplaces might bristle at being called intermediaries, but it is hard to argue that the 10 to 20 percent fee that they charge drivers and market participants isn't a monetary TxC dressed up in different clothes.

The TxCs that really matter are far more subtle and insidi-ous than the well-signposted financial charges of intermediaries. These TxCs can only be understood when one dives into the nitty-gritty of why a specific transaction is not taking place. It is easy to spot a transaction taking place; most people never stop to ask themselves why a transaction *isn't* happening. Remember: for each transaction or exchange that takes place there are countless (almost infinite) transactions that don't happen. This book is about the exchanges that never happened. Making exchange happen where the exchange was previously not possible, or even conceived of, is the essence of entrepreneurship.

For example, in the last chapter we looked at TxCs that lead men to only getting their hair cut every four to six weeks. Yes, there is an opportunity for entrepreneurs to improve the four-to-six-week haircutting experience, but the bigger opportunity is to drive up the frequency of haircuts. Yet if you ask men why they don't get their hair cut weekly or daily, they will likely roll their eyes at your stupidity. They cannot conceive a world of lower TxCs; they don't even know that they are beset by TxCs.

Entrepreneurial opportunities are completely obvious right after someone else captures them. Google, Etsy, Instagram, YouTube—all are no-brainers in hindsight.

I am hoping that by the end of this book you will start to look critically at the world through TxC glasses and ask yourself why transactions and exchange are not happening. TxCs are everywhere, waiting for entrepreneurs to crush them and make all sorts of new, currently inconceivable business models possible. A good place to start is with an understanding of the broad categories of TxCs that afflict everything we do, everything we might want to do, and everything we have no idea that we might want to do in the future until some entrepreneur makes it possible.

Exchange is blocked or inhibited by the following eight primary categories of TxCs:

1. **Inability to search the market.** If I can't find a customer or supplier at a good price, or if I only have limited knowledge of possible suppliers or customers, how can I find the best counterparty and do business comfortably?
2. **Lack of trust.** Parties that don't trust each other find it hard to do business together. The exception is where there is a fully functioning market operating between them that eliminates the need for trust.

3. **Tyranny of geography.** Living in Dublin, it is implausible for me to try to exchange with a barber in Turkey. At the micro-geographical level, I only exchange with the nearest coffee shop; I never exchange with the one 100 yards farther away. Geography matters a great deal.
4. **Inability to pinpoint a counterparty and close a contract.** Being able to search the market is useful, but if I can't pinpoint a specific supplier and close a deal with him or her, the exchange won't happen.
5. **Regulation and government protection.** Through a plethora of subsidies, tariffs, trade regulations, taxes, and so on, governments often feel the need to protect groups of suppliers or buyers from other, possibly better suppliers or buyers, thus blocking or inhibiting value-adding exchange.
6. **Lack of certainty in payment/transfer of value.** Money (value) does not normally travel on the same rails as a good or service. Someone might ship goods to me, but the payment goes on a separate rail, whether it is through a VISA/Mastercard process or a bank transfer process. Shipment might happen before payment, or payment might happen before shipment; the one who must jump first faces an uncomfortable risk TxC.
7. **Opportunity cost of people's time.** In the perfect world, I have a want and it is satisfied immediately. The elapsed two hours for me to go to the barber and back is a huge impediment to me getting my haircut. If two hours could be reduced to 15 minutes, I would get my hair cut a lot more often.
8. **Monetary TxCs.** Let's not forget them. They might be falling, but they have the resilience of the living dead and often come back to life in a new form!

o o o

Starting here and periodically throughout the book, I will review each of the eight major categories of TxCs in more detail.

TxC ONE:
INABILITY TO SEARCH THE MARKET

We need to be able to price-discover across the market and be highly confident that we are engaging in the best possible exchange. Without this confidence, we are hesitant to exchange.

EXPOSING ALL FLIGHT INVENTORY TO THE WEB

Those of us of a certain vintage remember the process of booking flights before the advent of the internet. We had to go into a travel agent's office or call them by phone to communicate our needs. Did they undertake a rigorous search to get us the best price, or did they just shift some poor flight inventory onto us in return for a nice little kickback from the airline? Was $500 the best price available or not? Did the agent consider that we were willing to take a two-legged flight rather than a direct flight?

Maybe we were only willing to pay $300 for the flight, and the airline only had a flight available for less than $300 at very limited times that the agent didn't think we would be interested in. We had to rely on our (conflicted) travel agent to find us the limited options, and, in many cases, they probably didn't, in which case valuable exchanges didn't happen. In summary, an inability to search the market leads to value-adding exchanges being thwarted.

Now, I can get onto a flight aggregation website and search for all the different combinations that might suit me. An extremely cheap middle-of-the-night flight from Los Angeles to Chicago with a layover in Miami for a few hours? Why not, if that's all that my budget can afford? I still might not be happy with the price and the itinerary, but at least I have the comfort that I have scoured the market rigorously and can exchange on this basis.

OPPORTUNITIES TO BRING SEARCH INTO ALL ASPECTS OF OUR LIVES

With the internet, if I want an apartment in Barcelona for four days or a ski apartment for a week, it is a simple as a few clicks, perusing some staged photos, reading the reviews closely to assess their authenticity, and clicking to contract with the owner or manager of the property. In the pre-internet era (and, to a large extent, pre-Airbnb) this was a monumental chore, and sometimes led to huge disappointments. Consumers had to go through an offline aggregation company, which took an outrageous cut.

The internet is opening more and more sectors to the ability to search the market, but many sectors remain untapped. Simple online search is only possible for tasks or products that can be defined relatively clearly. The internet (and falling TxCs) has commoditized certain previously complex purchase processes, such as booking a week in a chalet in Austria.

This leaves opportunities for entrepreneurs. Consider the following market search problems that entrepreneurs will solve in the future:

- **Expert home services:** Searching is still a problem for some transactions, such as picking a plumber for my leaky pipes. In the old days I would probably ask a neighbor or family member for a recommendation. I may have picked someone randomly from the phone book because their advertisement looked pretty decent, but then suffered through whatever low-quality service they inflicted on me. Now, I can get a comprehensive list of qualified plumbers in a few seconds through the internet, check out their reviews, and send them a message. But I still face the worry that I might have picked one that is unreliable.
- **Home extensions:** Even more challenging is a highly complex exchange such as trying to find a builder for an extension to my house. The level of TxC that goes into discussing my requirements with each builder (sharing

ideas, fleshing out costs, drawing plans, clarifying ambiguities, etc.) means that I can only engage with a very limited number of builders. I can end up fearful regarding my inability to search the market and the information asymmetry with my builder. The same goes for contracting with architects, interior designers, and so forth.

One person's problem is another person's opportunity. Entrepreneurs should not rest until they have brought forward propositions that thrill buyers and sellers with their ability to search the market perfectly.

TECHNIQUE C:
MULTIPLYING THE ABILITY TO SEARCH THE MARKET

In technique A we used the process of imagining perfection. In technique B, we looked for new business models built on driving up the velocity of customers' consumption. At various stages throughout this book, we will pick one individual category of TxC and see what sort of new propositions might be uncovered if we were able to eliminate that TxC—in this case, the TxC of being unable to search the market thoroughly.

In technique C we will explore entrepreneurial propositions that could be possible if entrepreneurs multiplied the ability for consumers and businesses to search the market. Where information asymmetry exists between buyers and sellers, the party that suspects it has an informational deficiency is naturally disinclined to exchange.

OUR ABILITY TO SEARCH THE MARKET HAS IMPROVED DRAMATICALLY

One of the first big benefits that the internet brought to economic activity was the ability to search across the market:

* eBay let us find all sorts of obscure stuff hitherto locked away in people's attics.
* Property listing sites put a lot of the information advantage of real estate agents into the hands of prospective home buyers.
* Fishermen could find out what prices could be achieved in nearby cities for their catch.
* Car buyers looking for a BMW 5 Series could find all those cars that were for sale in a particular region, whether being sold by dealers or private individuals. In the old days they probably relied on want ads in newspapers or car buyer magazines.
* Uber helped us to find nearby qualified drivers for hire.
* Etsy helped us to find the products of artisans and craftworkers.

There are still many opportunities for new business models targeting a better ability to search, even within sectors that already seem to have better-than-average search options.

EXPOSING EVERYTHING IN THE WORLD TO SEARCH

eBay and other listing sites have done a great job in helping some buyers to find items for sale that they might not otherwise have found, or helping some sellers to find buyers whom they might not otherwise have found. However, only a microscopic percentage of items in the world are available to be searched by potentially interested buyers and sellers.

For example, not one of the many items in my house is available to be searched by people who might want to buy one of them. I would hazard a guess that there is a US Civil War buff out there who might be interested in buying (or borrowing) my six-volume vintage biography of Abraham Lincoln, but she or he doesn't know that I have it and might be willing to sell it or let someone borrow it. How many times have I looked at an unused item in my house or garage and said to myself that I really must pass it along to someone who would value it more?

Remember: purely theoretically, in a perfect (no TxC) future, everything in the world would be exposed to the possibility of being searched. Not just the things in my house, but the things held by corporations, governments, charities, etc. If all the things in the world are to flow frictionlessly to the use case that delivers the highest value and happiness—like water from the high ground to the low ground—the first thing that needs to happen is that the things need to be findable. Without that, there is not the slightest chance of exchange happening.

Perfection, on the search front, is to have every product, service, asset, skill, etc. in the world, fully searchable in real time.

It is great that I can now find a secondhand BMW 5 Series on a car-buyer website from people who are, at this exact moment in time, willing to sell one, but what about the latent sellers who are only vaguely considering selling? Indeed, what about all the owners of such a car who are not considering a sale but might be enticed if the price is right and the process simple? A great entrepreneur needs to figure out a way to expose that product to a market search.

DELIVERING MORE "BROADBAND" SEARCH POSSIBILITIES

It has always been difficult to search across providers of complex services and products. Consider complex transactions such as getting a legal contract drawn up, procuring tax advice, or putting a house extension out for bidding to various builders. The quantity of data (and hassles in getting the data) required to do a proper search means that consumers and businesses are feeling their way through the dark when they want to engage a provider in these types of exchange.

The process for online search for expert services is still very nascent. Yes, if I need an expert to help me to set up a small trust for my kids, I can probably now get a list of possible tax advisors on the internet. But that list is not much use to me in my search. There is a big difference in skill set between a tax advice provider that deals with multinational transfer pricing issues and one that handles personal tax issues for individuals. Furthermore, the value difference between a great tax advice provider and a poorly skilled one is enormous. Unfortunately, the information we need is not available to us and we struggle to search for and differentiate the great from the poor. I am probably still going to call someone I know to get a referral.

Even for high value product categories such as houses and cars where the search process is more mature, the process can be unsatisfying. I can get a long list of secondhand car listings online for my impending purchase of a BMW 5 Series with the associated asking price, but I have no idea if the seller is reliable or has fiddled with the odometer. I have no idea of the real condition of the car engine or whether the car has been involved in a crash. Even for a product like a car, I can't simply search the market and press the "buy" button with confidence—that is the acid test of a perfect search process.

I need a much fuller "broadband" data set at my fingertips during the search process. Returning to the tax advice search process, a more perfect search capability would address issues such as:

- Are all the possible tax advisors listed?
- Are their fields of expertise fully delineated?
- How many times have they solved my problem before for other clients?
- Are there ratings or other mechanisms for sifting through the good and the bad advisors?
- Is there some way in which I can get visibility into the tax advisor's clients (in a disguised manner) and whether their clients have issues like my tax issues?
- Is there a mechanism for estimating the price for resolving my query?
- Is there a way to contract with the tax advisor?
- Can users of the platform get to the stage where they don't feel that they have imperfect information and feel that they can trust the platform?

The search propositions on the internet that we know and love today will evolve in the future to give more of a broadband view of the sellers and buyers aiming to participate in exchange. Furthermore, only a fraction of 1 percent of all the assets of the world are exposed to search on a real-time basis. The evolution of the market for search will deliver fantastic opportunities for entrepreneurs.

BRAINSTORMING ENHANCED SEARCH PROPOSITIONS IN SURGERY

Let's assume I need to have major back surgery that could have a profound impact on my life if it does not go well. A big problem I have is that there is complete information asymmetry between me and the people I deal with in the medical field. The decisions regarding my surgery are made by others; I am largely a mute passenger in the process.

I am hungry for information that might help me to make informed decisions that complement the medical expertise of the people I am dealing with. I would really like to know:

- How many of these specific back surgeries has this surgeon done before? Will the surgeon be performing the surgery, or will a junior surgeon who is only setting out on their career be learning by doing?
- What are the performance statistics of this surgeon? How does she or he compare to other surgeons in this hospital? What about surgeons in other hospitals within 100 miles? What about other back surgeons in the world? Am I getting an A-rated one?
- How competent are the rest of my medical team?
- What "service delivery failures" has this surgeon experienced in the past? Were there specific unforeseen or foreseen circumstances for those failures? Has he or she learned from past problems?
- How up to date is this surgeon with the latest treatment approaches? Is their approach considered best practice in the current environment?
- How much is this surgery likely to cost? Given my insurance plan, how much am I likely to have to pay?

There appears to be an expectation in the medical sector that performance statistics of different physicians should not be part of the process. However, this inhibits my ability to search and makes me a more nervous participant in the process.

o o o

The internet has not solved our search problems—it has barely scratched the surface. There may be better listing services for cars, houses, etc. than buying the evening newspaper and checking the want ads, but even the sectors that provide a reasonable search capability still offer relatively narrowband search capability and, more importantly, more than 99 percent of things in the world are not yet available to be searched.

Over the long term, the ability to perform a broadband search of all the relevant pieces of data will come to all aspects of exchange in which we engage. This will provide opportunities for our budding entrepreneurs, who could start by looking through every category of product and service and assessing whether a perfect search experience exists and, if it doesn't, how he or she could craft a dramatically improved search process.

CHAPTER 6

Transaction Costs Create "Just-in-Case" Home Lives

L et's start at home and explore how the current landscape of TxCs shapes the way that people live. The most mundane place in any home is probably the garage or the attic—the repositories of residual things. In the hierarchy of accessibility, the things currently on tables are probably the most accessible, then things within an arm's reach (e.g., waist level in the kitchen). This is followed by things put away in cupboards or on shelves, then things under beds, until we get to the bottom of the pile: things in the garage and attic.

For the purposes of this exercise, the most interesting things are at the bottom of the hierarchy, not our most here-and-now possessions. Picture my garage. It's probably not that different from many other garages around the world.

An electric scooter, purchased as a gift and ridden three times before childhood boredom kicked in. Half-full cans of paint used a few years ago in a frenzy of home improvement. A broad range of male must-have (but almost never used) power tools—a circular saw, a saber saw, two drills. Endless tools: wrenches, screwdrivers, nuts and bolts, nails, etc. No chainsaw due to fear of self-amputation, but lots of camping gear—a couple of tents, sleeping bags, camp stove. Three ladders, including a long one for cleaning upstairs windows and gutters (solely in theory, due to my fear of heights).

I could take you to my attic, jam-packed with boxes not opened since two house moves ago. Then to my kitchen full of useful appliances (including an iced tea maker and ice cream freezer—not used very often in Ireland) and stores of food, including every spice known to mankind. Then on to my home office where I am surrounded by 500-odd of my favorite books, laptops, a desk, a printer, old cameras, etc. This is probably not much different from the flotsam and jetsam accumulated throughout a normal life in many well-developed countries.

I did a quick calculation, and my guess is that I have 10,000 items in my house. But apparently, I am completely wrong: the average house has 300,000 items.* Though admittedly that is getting down to paper clips and envelopes, it is still an impressive number. Why do we have all this stuff?

LIVES WEIGHED DOWN BY INVENTORY

To borrow a phrase from the business world, why do people live their home lives drowning in inventory? The reason is TxCs.

The TxCs of having these items on hand are lower than the TxCs of not having them on hand. To pick one simple example: my hedge trimmer. The hedge trimmer gets used once a year, maybe twice if the hedge is lucky. I have made the (unconscious) choice that I am better off having a hedge trimmer in my garage on standby for occasional use for an hour or two per annum than not. In other words, I am willing to buy a hedge trimmer, absorb the depreciation over its useful life of 10 or so years, pay for the storage space in my garage, take the pain of the clutter, worry about the risk of robbery, pay insurance, etc. just to have it on hand (option A). An alternative would be the TxCs of driving to a garden equipment rental company (option B), paying the day rate for the rental, driving home, returning the hedge trimmer the following day, etc. Option C is that there surely must be someone in my neighborhood who has a hedge trimmer and who wouldn't

---

* Mary MacVean, "For Many People, Gathering Possessions Is Just the Stuff of Life," *Los Angeles Times,* March 21, 2014.

mind lending it to me for a nominal fee. But how do I find her? How does she build enough trust in me to lend the equipment? I might not return the item, or I might be a weirdo who shows up at her front door. In options B and C, there are many potential TxCs. The other alternative would be for me to hire someone I found on the internet to come to trim the hedge (option D), but then I need to face the challenges of searching for him or her, worrying about the fact they might be unreliable or late or criminal, supervising the work, maybe getting tricked over the price (did he forget to mention the call-out charge?), etc. I won't mention option E in which the neighbor's kid comes around to butcher the hedge (way too many TxCs).

Clearly, I have decided that it is easier to own rather than to rent or have someone come to trim the hedge. The TxCs of A are less than B, C, or D. Many of the TxCs of B and C are not much different from those associated with going to Blockbuster as described in Chapter 2. As you will have noticed again, most of the TxCs are not monetary: they are hassles or trust issues.

The exact same logic can be applied to every single item in people's lives: their books, their kitchen appliances, their clothes, their hairbrushes, their paper clips; their obscure spices used once in a recipe and never used again. We have all these things lying around just in case they might be needed at some stage in the future. As might be expected, in countries where storage space in homes is very limited, the quantity of things owned by people is dramatically reduced. The TxCs of ownership are just too high when the space is small.

Most of the time we don't think about these piles of inventory. Occasionally, we might start to scratch our heads about why on earth we live this way. The only time it comes to front of mind is when we are about to move house and we go through item by item, soul-searching regarding whether to keep or junk each possession.

Completely unsatisfactory though it is, we grudgingly admit that living in an inventory dump is generally the right thing to do given the current landscape of TxCs. It would be nonsense to have to rent a comb each time I need to use it. The TxCs would be overwhelming.

FALLING TxCS COAX US
TOWARD NON-OWNERSHIP

While ownership of most things is the default option, perhaps you might be able to stretch your brain to believe that, if it became easier to have a hedge trimmer delivered hassle-free into your hand on that one occasion in the year when you need it, and taken away when you finish, you might be willing to reconsider your rent-versus-buy decision. When you rent an item there's no need to store it, or charge it, or even to clean it. If the TxCs were to fall and the hassles of non-ownership abate, this rent-versus-own equation might start to tip the away from ownership.

We don't yet live in that world, and for all the things we own, there are lower TxCs to ownership today. Furthermore, most of us are blind to future possibilities. Most people are not able to look around the corner or even contemplate that we could do things differently. In the spirit of the Blockbuster example in Chapter 2, when we have a solution to our current needs that works, most of us are completely unable to conceive of alternative approaches. Why would we? The current approach meets our needs. Even to mention the benefits of renting a house brings out a chorus of moralizing about the societal benefits of home ownership and how young people can't get a foot on the home ownership ladder.

RENTING VERSUS SHARING

If non-ownership of everything we use becomes far more attractive as TxCs fall, are we heading toward a rentership economy, or a sharing economy? Will we get our hedge trimmer from a firm that rents out equipment in a very low-TxC manner, or will we see an explosion in the sharing economy, whereby we "borrow" it from our proverbial neighbor? The low economic marginal cost of the sharing economy should have an advantage as the purchase cost of the hedge trimmer has already been absorbed by the neighbor. In theory, the amortization of the cost of the hedge trimmer does not need to be shared across the neighbors that borrow it.

The advocates for the sharing economy are very vocal in support of "sharing" taking over the world. They may or may not be right. However, the firm that rents out the hedge trimmers as part of a professional business has some cards up its sleeve—it can potentially design a slicker (lower TxC) process for prospective renters. The objective is non-ownership in a low-TxC manner. Whether the hedge trimmer comes through a renter-ship or sharing economy model is a secondary question.

o o o

What does ownership versus non-ownership mean for entre-preneurs? Consumers (and businesses), whether they know it or not, are already making implicit trade-offs between owning and renting. At one end of the spectrum, when we go on our vacation to Spain, it would be financially nonsensical to buy a car instead of renting one. At the other end of the spectrum, it would be impractical to rent our raincoat—having it on hand for those rainy Dublin (or Seattle) days makes far more sense.

In the middle of this spectrum is the fruitful area for entre-preneurs to noodle around for new business propositions. The scale is progressively tipping toward non-ownership as TxCs fall and we can access more and more products and services on-demand. Indeed, many products are being turned into ser-vices by savvy entrepreneurs; we will discuss this further in Chapter 9.

TxC TWO:
LACK OF TRUST

If an inability to search the market is the first TxC that people and businesses typically encounter, the next TxC that gets in the way is usually a lack of trust.

Yes, we can search online for a tradesperson (such as a car mechanic or a boiler repair person) in a much more thorough way than we could in the past, but we still face the problem of trust. If the car mechanic can see from the blank look on my face that I haven't a clue what he is talking about when he mentions a problem with the hyperdrive, I suspect I am going to be facing a $2,000 replacement job rather than a $200 repair.

Lack of trust between the prospective partners to an exchange is by far the most destructive of all the TxCs. Excitingly, it is also the TxC category where a dramatic transformation is going on right now. Trust is spreading; it will release huge waves of entrepreneurial exchange between parties that didn't exchange in the past.

USING THE MARKET, BRANDS, OR CONTRACTS TO ENGENDER TRUST

If an exchange can be made through the mechanism of a well-functioning *market*, then the TxCs are essentially irrelevant. When buying a can of Coca-Cola from a shopkeeper or a street vendor, I don't need to have any trust in them. I don't need to know their reputation. I don't need to know if they just got out of prison for fraud. The only thing I need to know is the price of the can.

Separately, I have trust in Coca-Cola as it has spent decades building trust in its *brand*. A brand is a powerful but expensive mechanism for overcoming customer trust TxC issues. I have faith that my can of Coke has been produced in a clean environment and to the exact same formula that every other Coke can is made. Therefore, I am happy to exchange with the unknown street vendor for my Coke.

For transactions where trust between two parties is required over time but trust is currently limited, lawyers often come into the frame. The lawyers may come up with a *contract* (a set of rules) for governing the relationship between the two parties— when the goods will be delivered, credit terms, penalties for noncompletion, information rights, restricted transactions, etc. This contract is then monitored and enforced by a mutually agreeable court system or mediation process. In effect, we replace the TxC of lack of trust with a different TxC—the need to create a detailed set of binding rules. Perhaps over time, by working with one another, we can start to build trust in one another and reduce the need for contracts. Indeed, those people and organizations that use contracts in the initial stages of their relationship often find that they are barely referring to the terms of the contract once a certain level of trust builds up.

Contracts are only useful up to a point. They are very expensive to create and enforce. Furthermore, the power dynamics between the two parties can change over time. Imagine, for example, that I am a supplier of software to larger companies for managing their fleets of bus drivers. If I have a three-year contract, then I am in a powerful position at the end of the three years to get a renewal of the contract, as I will be the incumbent supplier with intimate knowledge of my customer's needs. I can take advantage of my position.

WHERE TRUST IS ESTABLISHED, EXCHANGE CAN FLOURISH

Most of us have at most two or three people whom we trust completely—with our savings, our homes, our families, our spouses, our thoughts. People are remarkably good at looking after their own interests; they don't seem to be quite as good at looking after other people's interests. We are right to hand out trust sparingly—many people don't deserve it.

Until recently, our ability to grant trust to someone was limited to whether we knew them personally, or someone that we trusted knew that person and trusted them. Other than that, trust was built up through reputation and branding or through repeated direct interactions. Counterparties earned our trust the hard way over time—only a very small number of people managed to jump through our trust hoop.

But if they did manage to jump through our trust hoop, their reward is the gift that keeps giving—we will exchange with them at a higher velocity rate. We will tell others how great (trustworthy) they are. Who hasn't breathed a sigh of relief at finally finding a car mechanic who talks car to us as a peer and isn't focused on finding innovative ways to charge us?

To see the power of trust, imagine that all 8 billion people in the world could be trusted fully, as opposed to the tiny number to whom we grant trust today. The quantity of exchanges in the world would grow at a logarithmic rate, and the value pools would explode. Trade would be unshackled as people would not be worried about payment terms or theft, or whether a delivery would show up. Everyone would automatically be a trusted supplier. Everyone could be a potential babysitter. People could just borrow my car and then drop it off when done. Our hedge trimmer exchange problem would disappear—I could leave my garage door open, and people could come and borrow whatever they liked. They could drop the $5 fee in a can, and I wouldn't have the slightest worry about the money being taken. It would be a nice world to live in.

It is not a surprise that high-trust societies tend to be highly successful economically.

TRUST INDICES

Maybe all 8 billion don't need to be completely trustworthy. A large number of exchanges with positive price space could be liberated with modest amounts of trust. I don't need to be able to place trust in everyone, as I don't come into possible exchange situations with them.

Maybe people and businesses could earn a *complete trust-worthiness* badge as if they were in the scouts. Then we would know who the trustworthy ones of the 8 billion are, and we could exchange just with them.

While this sounds far-fetched, some sort of trust measure for each person and business is a likely future node on the journey toward perfection. With vast and growing quantities of data on every person's and every business's behavior and powerful artificial intelligence algorithms, a trustworthiness index would not be too hard to construct. Indeed, primitive versions already exist in the data that drives credit scores for consumers and companies. Exchange will be skewed toward those with high scores.

The early versions of trust indices can be seen for services such as ride-sharing, temporary accommodation, and the various sharing economy propositions. A $100 billion ride-sharing sector has been built on the back of a trust index—the five-star rating (and the associated driver and passenger checks that the ride-sharing companies undertake). To let a stranger into one's car or to get into a stranger's car late at night based on a trust index is a truly remarkable achievement. If ride-sharing and other early sharing economy services have revolutionized their sectors using trust indices, there are many other fruitful sectors awaiting a similar overhaul.

SITUATION-SPECIFIC TRUST

Thankfully, to effect an exchange, we don't need to have complete trust in our counterparties along all dimensions; we only need to have trust that is specific to the exchange. Our "scout badges" can be granted for situation-specific trustworthiness dependent on the nature of the exchange:

- If I rent out my apartment on a holiday rental platform, I want to trust that the renters are not going to trash it.
- If I get into a car late at night, I want to trust that the driver is not going to do me harm or rip me off. The driver also wants to trust that I am a decent human who is not going to do him or her harm.

- If I hire someone to perform a personal service, I want to trust that they are not going to steal money or prove to be unreliable or show up late.
- If I let someone into my house to fix something, I want to trust that they are not scoping out the house for a later burglary.
- If I engage a psychotherapist, I want to know that they can maintain confidences.

All these exchanges require a high degree of situation-specific trust. That's a more manageable task than trying to build generalized trust.

INCREASING SITUATION-SPECIFIC TRUST

If the sharing economy is going to transform our world by taking advantage of all the unused things owned by people, companies, charities, governments, and other institutions, it will need a bedrock of trust that currently does not exist. While most of us appreciate the benefits of commerce in the internet-connected world, we fret about the potential fraud that seems to be inherent to the impersonal nature of the web. But new ways of building trust have been stealthily making inroads into our lives, and trust is being spread around in unexpected ways:

- **Reviews and ratings on a website by prior users of the service or service provider.** These have become incredibly important to us. The seller on eBay and the driver on Uber are keen to keep their ratings high as their trust index score is a valuable asset to them in their employment. Many people (and artificial intelligence algorithms) have, over time, become smart consumers of reviews and ratings. They try to discern the planted reviews, examine the service delivery failures carefully, and take comfort when the number of previous ratings is high.

- **Recommendations from a trusted third party, and in particular recommendations from someone we trust.** We are eager to try the restaurant that our friend raved about. Many of us have taken reference calls from people we know who see that we are connected to a certain person in our LinkedIn connection list.
- **One of the counterparties asking for a "hostage,"** e.g., the charge held or reserved against a credit card when booking a car. "Try and return" services are increasing; they use sophisticated algorithms to sort out the tire-kickers from the consumers who are likely to ultimately buy the products they try.
- **Personalization and effort expended by the supplier—** for example, a delightful write-up by a host on Airbnb that conveys the sense that he or she really cares about the quality of the experience they are delivering.
- **Know your customer checks.** These are becoming much easier in a connected world. We have to verify who we are when we open a bank account; in the future we will not be surprised to have to prove our identity when borrowing something from a neighbor. More trust in other people will increase exchange; our repair person will prove their identity when they show up to fix the plumbing.
- **Background checks of academic credentials, online work histories, and social media postings of prospective recruits.** Whether potential recruits like it or not, employers will have more trust in their hiring decisions by building a more expansive picture of the suitability of candidates without relying solely on résumés, interviews, and references from people who may lack objectivity.

○ ○ ○

So, how can entrepreneurs leverage trust to create new business propositions?

TECHNIQUE D:
SPRINKLING TRUST

In technique A for generating new entrepreneurial propositions, we looked for approaches using the process of imagining perfection. In technique B we looked for new business models built on driving up the velocity of customers' consumption. Technique C examined the first category of TxC—propositions for multiplying the ability to search the market.

In technique D we will explore propositions that could emerge if entrepreneurs had a magic bag of trust they could deploy to let buyers and sellers exchange in situations where they wouldn't otherwise trust each other.

TRUST PROBLEMS ARE UBIQUITOUS

In this chapter we covered how lack of trust is one of the most debilitating of TxCs, blocking out large quantities of potential exchange. It also skews exchange in favor of insiders and incumbents, which is not good for the health of our societies and economies.

It is easy in a brainstorming session to develop a long list of situations where the world is beset by trust problems:

- Immigrants to a country can struggle to get good jobs as their qualifications are not understood, so they can't generate the required trust among employers.
- Former convicts often suffer from challenges in finding employment.
- People and companies in the West who want to source products in Asia or other geographies with which they are not familiar are often asked for letters of credit or up-front payment.
- An unknown neighbor might want to borrow or rent my hedge trimmer for the day.
- A teenager might want to take a job in a restaurant but may be worried about her or his safety walking home from the restaurant late at night.

- A vender of household appliances might struggle to build a business without offering credit to unknown consumers.
- Tenants need to convince landlords that they will treat the property well.

While a budding entrepreneur can come up with a list of ideas if we look at places where trust is lacking, on examination there are enormous swathes of the economy beset by trust issues just waiting to be solved by entrepreneurs. These include:

Sharing economy businesses: the 300,000 items in a house and the umpteen occasionally idle pieces of equipment within companies are crying out for someone to bring trust and allow them to be exposed to the sharing economy.

Personal services and trades delivered by sole traders rather than by branded chains of service providers are often hampered by trust issues. These sole traders would probably benefit from being part of a swarm or association that offers their customers trust indices, with processes in place to ensure consistency in standards of work across the members of the swarm. (We will discuss swarms more in Chapter 13.)

Major works that take place over time, like getting an attic conversion or an extension in one's home, are stressful—one feels unmoored in an unfamiliar land where trust levels can be very low (and rightfully so). Architects, builders, and their clients understand that the day the contract to undertake the work is signed, power passes from the client to the architect and builder.

WHERE TO FIND A MAGIC BAG OF TRUST?

An entrepreneur that can engender trust between a buyer and seller at scale (beyond the scope of personal relationships) has the key ingredient for a fantastically valuable business. Where and how might the entrepreneur look for a magic bag of trust-enhancing techniques on which to build her business? There are many ways:

- **Form self-regulating groups.** Turn a group of individually untrusted sellers or buyers into a self-regulating swarm of sellers or buyers who are highly incentivized to conform to the swarm's norms. Think of the types of benefits that a franchise model supplies.
- **Provide a qualified referral service.** One of the most common uses of LinkedIn is to cross-reference a potential counterparty by contacting someone you know in common.
- **Front a guarantee.** It might be possible for an entrepreneur to put himself in the middle of a transaction financially to guarantee the actions of one of the parties.
- **Put together a review and ratings system** that crowdsources perspectives on groups of suppliers that are relatively untrusted to date.
- **Act as a type of insurance company** to guarantee the good behavior of parties to different types of transactions.
- **Create narrowband trust indices** specific to certain types of exchange.

WHAT OPPORTUNITIES COULD BE UNLOCKED BY TRUST?

Let's take the last type of magic bag of trust from the section above—narrowband indices of trust relevant to a specific type of exchange. Let's brainstorm consumer propositions that would be unlocked by a reliable trust index. Remember, the entrepreneur doesn't need to run all the operations of the business—they might just be able to supply the trust, in instances such as:

- A dog-walking service that comes to my house (with keys to my house) to pick up the dog for an hour in the middle of the day
- A childcare service offered by people in their homes
- Being the executor of someone's will after they have died
- Going to the bank or the driver's license facility on people's behalf
- Managing the money of elderly people with dementia
- A system for vetting people who interact with children or vulnerable adults
- A streamlined bail system

This could involve trade between two continents where the parties don't know each other. It could be to close the time gap between when a supplier has to provide goods or services and when he or she gets paid for those goods or services.

o o o

As you have seen, trust is a powerful TxC that blocks much exchange. Within this chapter we have covered how new techniques for trust enhancement are becoming possible. Entrepreneurs can use these new techniques to solve challenges that were previously intractable.

CHAPTER 7

Transaction Costs Shape Our Lives

You have seen how the architecture of our home lives is shaped by TxCs. TxCs influence whether we own and keep certain items in the house or whether we rent them. They also shape the exact spot where we keep those items in the house—are they directly on a table, or stored in a wardrobe, or buried in a box in the attic?

We put things where the aggregate TxCs to us are lowest. We have a set of unconscious mathematical equations in our heads for determining the exact place for each item; there is order behind seeming chaos. My socks go in the wardrobe in the bedroom beside my underwear, whereas my coat goes in a hallway closet near the front door—obvious and completely sensible of course, reducing my TxCs.

But TxCs are in the eye of the beholder: no wonder there are marital disputes about housework. Why wouldn't yesterday's newspaper be on the couch waiting for me to do the crossword, even though someone else wants it in the recycle bin? Her TxCs and mathematical equations are different than mine. I would like to throw out all the paint cans in the garage, whereas she goes for an expansive view of the ownership-on-demand model, just in case the walls take a few knocks over the next 5, 10, and 20 years. If only there were an on-demand paint delivery service that delivered micro-pots of paint with a blockchain-like record of all the paint combinations used in my house over the years! Then our TxCs structures might come into alignment. I am starting to see a new business opportunity in couples' therapy—solving marital problems through her and his mutual TxC understanding and alignment. "It's not you; it's my TxCs."

THE ARCHITECTURE OF OUR ENTIRE LIVES

When we look beyond our home, we realize that the same shaping influence of TxCs pervades our lives and our behavior.

For example, the opportunity cost of our time is a major determinant of where we live. We all undertake a complex calculus of the travel distances for the different aspects of our lives. Maybe I am willing to endure a work commute of 30 minutes each way, and the kids can handle a 20-minute bus ride or walk, but a major grocery store should be no more than three miles away, and I want my elderly parents no more than a 30-minute drive away. Minimizing the weighted-average aggregate TxCs of these journeys is a major determinant to where we live, overlaid with questions as to affordability, niceness of the neighborhood, sufficiency of space, etc. A new fast train or express bus lane that reduces these times (TxCs) can widen the boundaries of my search area and ultimately change the shape of the city.

TxCs also affect who we marry. In the world before online dating, the TxCs of meeting a partner were much higher as the ability to search across a wide variety of potential partners was completely stunted. One ran into potential partners at social events with friends, at work, through an introduction from a mutual acquaintance, or through a family-arranged connection. Now a willing partner can search across a much vaster network of prospective spouses. Some studies suggest that up to 39 percent of couples are now finding each other online, whereas those who meet at work are down to 11 percent of the total. People can also search across much wider geographies. Unfortunately, this broader market also means we run into another TxC, the *tyranny of geography*—we might spot and meet the ideal partner online, but he or she might live on the other side of the country. Who knows how this enhanced ability to search, magnified by the internet, will play out over the long term?

While American teenagers might think nothing of apply-
ing to colleges across the North American Continent, things are
different in other parts of the world. In Europe, for example,
almost all students attend undergraduate programs in their
home country. This might be for the prosaic reason that going
locally saves a lot of cost due to the ability to live at home, but
it is also in large part due to the nonmonetary TxCs of going
abroad. People don't know the reputation of the various colleges
in other countries or the specific programs in those colleges.
Indeed, people have little idea of the paperwork required to apply
abroad. Employers in the home country find it hard to understand the skill set the student has acquired from an unfamiliar
university. Anyone who looks at the situation will probably agree
that over the coming years, a higher percentage of students will
attend college abroad in Europe. It will become easier to apply,
and the reputation of the better programs will become more
widely known; employers will begin to seek out students from
across the Continent. The TxCs will decline, and soon it will be
as natural for a student from Ireland to go to college in Vienna as
it will be to attend the nearby college in Dublin. It is easy to see
possible business models for entrepreneurs to exploit this shift
over time. In the United States there is already an industry built
up around helping students get into different colleges, wherever
they are located.

o o o

As TxCs continue to fall, all fundamental aspects of our lives—
where we live, where we go to college, where we vacation, and
so forth—are up for grabs, with major effects on value pools.
Entrepreneurs who can understand the shifting landscape of
TxCs can anticipate the impact on people's lives and be one step
ahead of everyone else in delivering exciting propositions.

For example, Covid-19 accelerated the move to working from
home as technologies such as videoconferencing, collaboration
software, and fast broadband reduced the TxCs of not coming to
the office. What if some bright entrepreneur reduces the opportunity cost of my commuting time by making me as productive
working from my car as I am from home or in the office?

TxC THREE:
THE TYRANNY OF GEOGRAPHY

THE EXCESS SUPPLY/EXCESS DEMAND CONUNDRUM

Excess demand and excess supply are not expected to coexist; the two lines are supposed to cross and set the price. Unfortunately, Economics 101 often glosses over the reality that, most of the time, people who want a need fulfilled are not in the same place as those who are in position to fulfill that need.

On the demand side, my needs are simple; yet most of the time they are unfulfilled. My office is half an hour walk from home (what a TxC annoyance!). A warm beach is at least a flight away. I would love to live in a wonderful apartment in Buenos Aires overlooking the river delta—the only problem is that it would be a very awkward and tiring high-TxC commute to Dublin on a daily or even weekly basis, not to mention the cost. The nearest coffee shop is 400 yards away from me in Dublin; that's why I have invested in a good coffee maker. The bottle bank that collects bottles for recycling is 10 minutes' drive away, so empty bottles stack up in boxes until the garage is overflowing with them.

On the other side of the equation, there are endless suppliers across every sector who are keen to serve my needs, but they are in the wrong place! That excellent house painter from Latvia I saw on the internet charges half what I would pay her peer here in Dublin, but she is over there and my house is here. We suffer from overpriced housing in Dublin, but there are wonderful houses awaiting me in other places that are just too far away for me to commute. It is great that my thorough internet search turned up a trustworthy driver for my occasional evening out, but he is based too far away—it is not worth his time driving more than 15 minutes to service my demand. Even at this microlevel, geography gets in the way.

Excess supply of a good or service in one place and excess demand for the same good or service somewhere else is the tyranny of geography TxC. If we could only match up this supply and demand and zap these TxCs, endless new pools of exchange and value would gush forth. In the meantime, we have under-rewarded suppliers and unfulfilled customers.

To borrow a well-worn phrase, the world is becoming a smaller place. While the tyranny of geography now often blocks exchange, the world has an inbuilt entrepreneurial dynamic for closing gaps that can release value. Let's look at the ways this simultaneous excess supply/excess demand conundrum is being tackled progressively over time.

SOLVING EXCESS SUPPLY/DEMAND 1: MOVEMENT OF GOODS

A few centuries ago, the ability to exchange goods was severely constrained due to poor transportation options. Trade was hyper-local, and value surpluses and opportunities for entre-preneurs were consequently tiny. Over time, new low-cost transportation modes such as canals and trains emerged and prosperity was spread to regions where excess potential supply had been bottled up.

For example, when the US Erie and Ohio canals were built and train networks began to spread in the United States, farm-ers in Ohio and other newly accessible regions were able to get their goods to the excess demand New York market faster and cheaper, and a boom in trade from Ohio ensued.

Over time, advances in transportation have joined up all sorts of excess supply with areas of excess demand. It is worth-while to step back and reflect on some of the exchanges that now take place and marvel at the smooth-running supply chains:

- Flowers are grown in Kenya and other African countries and flown into the European market.
- Fruit for the European market comes from South Africa and Israel.
- Sandwiches for the lunchtime market can be made in one country (or state in the United States) for sale and consumption in another.

• We think nothing of ordering a box of paper clips online for a few dollars and have them show up in the mail from China or Vietnam.

Some people might criticize the externality costs such as climate impact of this globalization; flying flowers between continents sounds over the top. But the benefits to the people living in opportunity-poor labor areas of excess supply regions such as Kenya can be stunning. In the past, those workers would not have been able to capture any value other than what they could attain in their local market. Now, by injecting their labor into goods and moving those goods to where they are in demand, workers from less prosperous regions have the potential to capture more value. Clearly, in the absence of good regulation there is a danger that workers might be subject to exploitative labor practices, but one answer to this problem is for the excess supply in those regions to be fully utilized so that the increased demand drives higher wages and workers capture more of the value of their efforts.

SOLVING EXCESS SUPPLY/DEMAND 2: MIGRATION

Another way to solve the excess supply/excess demand conundrum is for migration to be allowed. Free movement of people within the European Union is a good example of ways of boosting exchange that wouldn't otherwise happen. Labor previously locked up in one country can now find a market for itself in other European countries. Witness the fabled Polish plumber who is happily exchanging his skills with households in France, Ireland, and elsewhere.

A more complicated situation arises when there is an excess pool of labor in a geography that is next door to wealthy markets where supply is limited and often protected by restrictive labor laws. Both the United States and Europe are adjacent to regions with enormous amounts of under-rewarded supply and labor that is desperate to match itself up to the sources of excess demand in those wealthy markets. Excess supply is very effective at finding its way to market.

SOLVING EXCESS SUPPLY/DEMAND 3: SERVICES DELIVERED REMOTELY

Services were incredibly difficult to deliver remotely prior to the advent of inexpensive and highly functional telecommunications and information systems. Now, any service that can be digitized—software development, PowerPoint preparation, logo design, proofreading, etc.—can transcend the tyranny of geography. It is an enlightening experience to sketch some PowerPoint presentation pages one evening, email them to someone in a distant country who works on them overnight at an hourly rate, and have them show up as highly professional pages early the following morning.

We are right at the bottom of a growth S-curve of exchange regarding the delivery of remote services. As we move up this S-curve, the release of new forms of exchange will lead to major pools of value (and major disruptions in labor markets in excess demand countries). The excess supply/excess demand equation for these sorts of services has an immensely long way to go before these markets start to operate efficiently.

There are some obvious examples of digitizable services where the growth in exchange can only go up. For instance, consider online education. A language teacher is already sitting in Bogotá explaining *el subjuntivo* in Spanish grammar to someone in Russia over a videoconferencing service. As will be discussed later in the book, a complete remake of teaching at undergraduate level is surely impending, not just because it could be fundamentally cheaper, but also to access and develop the skills of promising students around the world. Why is the world's best skyscraper design engineer teaching 50 students in his or her university? Why isn't he or she teaching all of the students in the world interested in such a subject? Why should the bright student in Nepal be blocked from a great MIT engineering education when it could be offered to him or her remotely on a nominal marginal-cost basis?

In contrast, due to regulation (and customer inertia), banks are tied to specified legal and regulatory jurisdictions. While regulation and the tyranny of geography can be limiting TxCs in the short run, the fundamental economics of a situation tend to do an end run around the attempts of regulators to block certain types of excess supply meeting excess demand. One would not be making a particularly insightful prediction regarding the future of financial services to suggest that they will get equalized across geographies over time. It is clearly nonsense that mortgage borrowers (with similar credit profiles) and savers face materially different mortgage and deposit rates in different countries in the Eurozone. New fintechs will capture the opportunity if the incumbents don't get there before them.

SOLVING EXCESS SUPPLY/DEMAND 4: THE HARD CASE OF LOCAL SERVICES

Now we get to the hard nut of services that (currently) need to be delivered in person. An eager house painter based in some far-flung country would need to come to Dublin to paint my walls. I am struggling with the logistics of how to get the walls of my house sent to him.

It is hard to see how some types of services can be delivered—a hyper-local presence is still required. I can't get my hair cut through the internet, or my house cleaned, or my garden dug. Forget about globalization of these services; I need to find someone very local—providers won't want to travel more than, say, 15 or 20 minutes. Often, they will want to charge a call-out cost to cover their travel—a geography TxC—before they even start to do any work.

Is there any way geography can be overcome for these services? From where we sit today, nothing obvious comes to mind. The short answer may that these services will just have to be delivered locally; it is hard to foresee technological advances that might change this.

But, as we discussed earlier, the excess supply—the pool of available service suppliers in one place—that is prevented by geography from meeting the demand for services from people in another is like steam building up in a kettle. Excess capacity tends to find its way to market, particularly when marginal cost economics can be exploited.

SOLVING THE LAST MILE PROBLEM

Most of the discussion of the tyranny of geography so far has been about very large distances, often international. There is a much more prosaic local geographical problem that, when solved, will yield a wave of entrepreneurship. Unlocking the potential power of the sharing economy and other entrepreneurial opportunities will require the ability to get things to and from people in their homes and offices in a very low-TxC manner. This is the last mile (or last 1,609 meters) problem.

For example, if I decide to offer up all the tools in my garage for sharing with my neighbors, I am going to need a third party that can overcome the TxCs associated with getting the things from person to person and back again. Without this, the proposition is likely to fail. The same problem exists for firms getting products to people and back again (e.g., from the hardware store to the person doing home repairs who urgently needs a three-inch bolt).

This last mile problem needs to be solved to unplug vast quantities of exchange. Lots of entrepreneurs are nibbling at parts of this problem, but there is no one yet that is close to solving it. At some stage, the last mile will be an integrated, on-demand service as simple as plugging an electric cord into a socket. It probably will be multimodal, involving walkers, bicyclers, motorcyclists, and drivers. It probably will be multi-nodal, involving shops, gas stations, homes, businesses, and drop-off points. It will be smart with dynamic routing, predictive demand, real-time tracking, and built-in redundancy.

The last mile solution might be one branded player; it might be many players, or even a fully disaggregated swarm coordinated by an open-source platform. Whatever it is, it will become a TxC-crushing platform that will get things to and from homes and businesses seamlessly. This will have a profound impact on exchange and kick off a new wave of entrepreneurship that is panting on the sidelines waiting for this problem to be solved.

In the last two techniques, we looked at propositions that could emerge if we could "turn off" a specific TxC. In the case of technique C, it was to solve the problem of the inability to search the market, and in technique D, it was lack of trust between possible counterparties to an exchange.

In technique E, we will look the problem of the tyranny of geography. We will do this by hunting for situations where there is excess supply and excess demand in the market simultaneously due to geographical gaps, and then considering whether there are ways to bridge these gaps and match up the excess supply to the excess demand.

GEOGRAPHY IS THE ENEMY OF EXCHANGE

In the last section, you saw how the impact of geography decreasing over time. Goods can be shipped from remarkable locations (such as flowers from Kenya). Migration is increasing. Digitizable services such as legal advice, design services, and proofreading can now be delivered by suppliers in all four corners of the world to buyers similarly dispersed. While these markets are still nascent, we can all foresee a future in which these global markets for digitizable services operate frictionlessly. Indeed, arbitraging skills and labor rates across locations will lead to a large realignment of economic activity between countries and regions, and perhaps will prove to be a primary engine for value creation in the world over the next decade or two, while potentially causing major disruption among existing suppliers.

While these are admirable examples of entrepreneurs overcoming geography, exchange that involves some physical dimension often doesn't occur due to geography:

* It is still too far for me to go and get an ice cream every time the urge strikes me.

- I might really like the excellent pints of beer at my favorite pub, but it is a mile from my house and delivery of draught beer in pint glasses is still a nascent business.
- The barber I like best is trumped by three closer barbers.
- People in my part of the city might be willing to share their lawnmower with me, but if they are more than a few hundred yards away, we probably can't exchange, absent a much better last mile delivery capability.
- I would be thrilled if that Italian tiler, whose work I loved seeing on my recent vacation, could get to Ireland to tile my bathrooms.

In each of these cases we have a supplier with excess capacity who is keen to meet my needs, and we have a willing buyer. We just can't match them up given the landscape of TxCs that currently exists.

DISAGGREGATION WILL HELP TO SOLVE THE CONUNDRUM

Geography will always be a problem for exchange that has a physical aspect. But there is a way forward for getting around the geography problem that will be enabled by falling TxCs. *Falling TxCs facilitate the disaggregation of tasks.*

What does disaggregation of tasks mean? Every job entails a series of tasks. A carpenter who has been commissioned to install a built-in wardrobe has to come to the house, discuss the need with the homeowner, measure the space, procure the materials, schedule the work, and install the wardrobe. She will undertake all these tasks herself.

If disaggregated, each of these tasks could, in theory, be undertaken by a different person and even a different firm. What stops them from being undertaken by different people today is TxCs. The TxC of coordinating the work and passing the task down the line to the next person is simply too high. It is easier if one person does all the work. Time would be wasted with different providers coming back and forth.

Hopefully you can see that, if the TxCs fall, it might start to make sense for the tasks to start getting disaggregated. The master carpenter might be truly talented at the actual building and installation of the wardrobe, but maybe she doesn't need to undertake the lower value (and time-consuming) tasks like measuring the space accurately, buying the right pieces of wood, and cleaning up the mess afterward.

Disaggregation leads to value creation on several dimensions. It means that the best people at different tasks can be assigned to each task. The time of the scarce resource (the master carpenter) can be used optimally. It also means that some of the tasks might become susceptible to being undertaken by software. The more tasks are broken down to their basic elements, the more likely that software can take over the task, offering the potential for enormous productivity gains. In our wardrobe example, the design of the wardrobe could easily be done by software with input provided by the homeowner.

We will explore more on the subject of disaggregation in Chapters 16 and 17, but here I will give one more example.

DISAGGREGATION OF THE GARDEN LANDSCAPING BUSINESS

Take, for example, the job of turning my garden from a hayfield into a place of Zen relaxation. I want to do something special with my garden. I have searched the web and identified a great garden landscaper in Osaka, Japan. He is the perfect person to create my new Zen-inspired garden.

In the past I would not even have been able to discover him due to an inability to search the market. I would have struggled to communicate with him and build trust—never mind the obvious geographical challenge, since he is thousands of miles away. The TxCs associated with working with him would have made the exchange unthinkable.

As the years go by and TxCs fall, the possibility of working with him will increase. The key driver will be the fall in the TxCs that make it possible to disaggregate the job efficiently into more individual tasks; we must then figure out which of these tasks my garden master needs to do himself, and which ones must be done locally. The garden job might be disaggregated into the following tasks:

- **Measurement of the garden**—maybe by the homeowner, or over time by technology
- **Working through designs**—by the Japanese landscaper, leveraging collaboration software
- **Clearing the site**—by local labor, maybe contracted through a gig economy platform
- **Purchase of the plants and any required hardware**—done by the homeowner, under supervision of the landscaper (or maybe in collaboration between the landscaper and a local garden center)
- **Installation of landscaping and planting**—locally hired labor, supervised by the homeowner
- **Supervision of the project**—the Japanese landscaper

In effect, the Japanese landscaper becomes the master coordinator and will accrue the highest value in the exchange, compared to the others who are simply offering their (supervised) labor.

○ ○ ○

While it might seem like it is not possible to overcome the TxC of geography for personal and non-digitizable services, once the personal service is disaggregated into its constituent parts, new forms of exchange may become possible. Furthermore, as software undertakes more and more of the high value aspects of these exchanges, the delivery location of these services can be progressively disaggregated from the physical location of the person or business on the receiving end of the service.

CHAPTER 8

The Journey Toward the Zero-TxC World

What do consumers and businesses ultimately want? Thankfully, this is a very easy question to answer. We want zero TxC fulfilment of our wants and needs. We want everything—absolutely everything—to be available to us on-demand. Entrepreneurial business propositions that move us in this direction have the chance of succeeding.

But zero-TxC fulfilment of our wants and needs is still in the relatively distant future for many aspects of our lives. The question for entrepreneurs today is how they can offer propositions that take consumers and businesses directionally toward the future of zero TxCs while recognizing the reality of the world as it is today and will be in the short to medium term.

WHAT WOULD MY LIFE BE LIKE IN THIS FUTURE ZERO-TxC WORLD?

I feel godlike: simply with the click of a finger, or by pressing a button on a phone, or ultimately just thinking about it, things happen—my needs and wants are fulfilled. Even better, my needs and wants are anticipated and fulfilled automatically.

Hedge, be cut! Driver, show up at 10:05 at my driveway! Teeth, be clean! Ice cream, be in my fist and ready for consumption! Walls, be painted! Rice, be made and ready to merge with the chicken curry at 6:40 p.m.! Chin, be shaved! Dirty dishes, be done!

Everything in the world would be available to me in a perfectly on-demand manner into which I plug effortlessly. Everything would be as easy as plugging into a socket to get electricity. It is a limitless existence; my hassles are gone.

I would own absolutely nothing; possessions are traps laden with TxCs. I wouldn't own the car that currently sits in my driveway, or even the house that I live in. In theory, I might not even know where I am going to be sleeping tonight. In true extremis, I might not even own the clothes on my back. Clothes would show up, right when I need or want them. It's difficult to conceive, but people may come to the realization that they don't need to own things. What they want is the benefit that the thing gives.

People don't want a camera—they want access to the memories inherent in the images. Instead, we have dusty albums full of physical photos and digital albums that are rarely accessed. Someone who figures out how to deliver these memories to me seamlessly will win out my business over the company that just wants to sell me a camera or a digital repository for images.

A zero-TxC world would be completely on-demand and just-in-time. And, for some aspects of it, this is infinite years away. Yet that's the direction that we are going. How will this happen? I don't know—but some smart entrepreneur might figure it out.

This book is about entrepreneurship rather than theoretical abstracts about infinite years hence, but it is critical to know what the end-point nirvana looks like. Entrepreneurs can now get busy taking us on the journey in that direction. There's opportunity and value to be captured on the way, and entrepreneurs just need to follow the signposts pointing out the falling TxCs.

WHERE ARE WE ON THE JOURNEY TOWARD ZERO TxCS?

In Chapter 3, we looked at some examples where we already live in a highly on-demand world. Most of the world's information and content is one tap away on a search engine, so access to information and facts is no longer a constraint on our lives. In most of the Western world, our gas, water, and electricity show up endlessly, in exactly the places where we want them. Your reaction may be, "Well, those areas are fundamentally differ-ent from the rest of life, the real world." Utility services have been on-demand for decades, and information, books, music, and video are digitizable and that makes them easy to deliver on-demand.

The on-demand phenomenon is colonizing many more fac-ets of our existence. We can access an army of drivers on Uber and its competitors. Today, it might seem like we are ordering a driver. Over time, as the network of drivers becomes denser and essentially ubiquitous, it will feel like we are accessing a liquid inventory of drivers that flows to where it is needed most. It is highly conceivable that, over the medium term, we will move wholesale toward "renting" rather than owning cars through the medium of ride-sharing, especially if self-driving cars take off.

The world's accommodation and virtually all travel and hospitality services are far easier to search across and contract with than in the past. The flight inventory of the world is at my fingertips waiting to be booked. Every accommodation option, whether a hotel room, a rental apartment, a hostel bed, a tent site, or a spare room in someone's house, can be booked online.

The services of all sorts of workers are available online. Take a task such as designing a logo for a law firm; in the old days, I was stuck with whatever local marketing and design talent I happened to encounter. Now I can search the global market (a major TxC relaxed) and pinpoint and contract with (another TxC relaxed) the ideal person who developed logos that I like for other law firms. I can pay simply, through PayPal, Venmo, Revolut, and other services (another TxC relaxed). It could be the designer himself who went to the bother of reducing my TxCs, or the online service he signed up with that has made an intensive effort to crush the TxCs facing me. Either way, logo development is starting to feel like a service that I can plug into relatively seamlessly (and unplug if need be). This analogy clearly stretches to many other tasks as well.

But even these services are a long way from being truly on demand. With true on-demand, I barely need to think of something and my want is met. Ride-sharing is great, but I want my car right now—not in two minutes—even though my meeting ended five minutes early.

Where are we on the TxC-reduction journey? We have barely started. Our cadre of aspiring entrepreneurs needs to get cracking to address my wants with more on-demand, zero-TxC services!

"BUT WHAT ABOUT . . ." OBJECTIONS

This world of the distant future with zero TxCs and no ownership sounds somewhat cold and functional. Isn't there something special about sleeping peacefully in *my* own bed? Living surrounded by *my* favorite books? Sitting in *my* comfortable chair?

Relax; no one is going to force you to do anything, nor to own nothing. If the TxCs are lower for you to own those things rather than fulfilling your wants via an on-demand service, then you will own them.

For example, someone might say that she enjoys the sheer aesthetic pleasure of seeing the full set of leather-bound Charles Dickens novels on her shelf and owning them gives her a certain self-satisfied feeling that can't be replicated by reading the books on an e-reader. Currently, the written word on a page can be so much more enjoyable than reading on a screen. Clearly that feeling is a strong transactional benefit to that person, but perhaps it could be overcome if, by clicking her finger or a button on a website, she could have a first edition of *Great Expectations* signed by the great man nestled in her hand right at the time that she is curling up on a sofa designed for reading that itself just magically arrived. Is this sort of capability currently possible? No, but that is why we have entrepreneurs—they are the ones who need to figure out when and how it might be possible to do away with the TxCs preventing our Dickens reader from curling up on the specially designed sofa with a prized first edition.

Books, incidentally, are a good example of the progressive tipping of the scales away from ownership in recent years. A large inventory of books used to be almost an interior decorating must-have and a social signal of eruditeness. Now, for many people, e-readers are leading to a shedding of books, and secondhand books are losing value.

THE OWNERSHIP MODEL IS APPALLINGLY WASTEFUL

Many of us are familiar with the following setting: a beloved parent or cherished uncle dies, and the family members left behind have to deal with the fallout. One of the most depressing things that must be done is to sort out all the treasured possessions of the departed. The family looks through the belongings and takes the old photos and a few pieces with vivid memories attached to them. Then an estate buyer might come through and chose a vintage sideboard and some crystal.

The other 95 to 99 percent goes to a charitable resale shop or the landfill. No one in the family wants the beds bought at an antiques auction, the sofa bought for $5,000, the coffee cups that departed parents used for the last 30 years of their lives, the porcelain place settings from the wedding decades or generations earlier. Not to mention books, rugs, and old tools, jars of assorted nails, and ancient camping gear from the garage.

Our descendants will look back at our inventory dumps and shake their heads. My unfortunate hedge trimmer should have become the proud cutter of hundreds of hedges every year and retired to appliance heaven content with having been a productive member of society. Instead, the manufacturers of the hedge trimmers might be forgiven if they designed hedge trimmers to be good only for a small number of uses throughout their life.

For now, my hedge trimmer lies in my garage, in imagination as unhappy as a dog that isn't taken for a walk. We wastrels are only being rational; our inventory dumps currently make sense for us. But this is changing.

TxC FOUR:
INABILITY TO PINPOINT A COUNTERPARTY AND
CLOSE A CONTRACT

After searching the market to identify possible exchange partners, it would be ideal if the willing buyer (or seller) would be able to pinpoint the best counterparty and close a contract with them. Uber, for example, allows me to pinpoint the nearest available driver and to contract with him or her for the service to get me where I want to go. The app allows me to do all this in a tiny-TxC manner—all I need to do is push a button. I don't need to worry about the terms and conditions in the contract or the pricing; I can just close the deal. This ability to pinpoint and close can drive up the quantity of exchange. In a perfect world, the provider would anticipate my impending need for a ride without me alerting it and the car would just show up to where it needs to show up. No doubt ride-sharing companies are thinking about this.

Pinpointing might involve finding the cheapest, the highest quality, the one in whom one can place the most trust, etc. With the magic of GPS, it can be the one closest to where you are. Perhaps it can be a combination of setting criteria and then pinpointing the nearest counterparty that meets the criteria.

People want the ability to contract directly—for example, if I want to use a beauty or hair salon, in many cases I can simply go straight into their booking system and pick the time that works best for me. Not being able to contract directly in some sort of straight-through process is a real inhibitor to exchange. Imagine I spent a few dreamy hours surfing Airbnb and looking at staged photos only to find that I then needed to email the hosts and see if they had availability, and then later to pin down the booking, and later again to make a payment. This would be a big drag on the exchange. People also want to have price transparency, if possible.

The ability to pinpoint a counterparty and close a contract easily already exists in a number of areas:

- Uber and other ride-sharing services
- Airbnb and other accommodation providers
- Air travel and rail travel

In other areas, this ability does not yet broadly exist:

- Household services (furnace repair and servicing, painting, gardening, window cleaning, plumbing, gutter clearing)
- Personal services (teeth cleaning, dental work, dog grooming)
- Professional services (real estate sales and leasing, will preparation, investment advice)

For many of these tasks we don't have the ability for users to make a straight-through booking. We can't simply pick a time that suits us. We can't agree on a fixed price before providers start work, as the scope of the work is ambiguous.

Entrepreneurs are probably working on propositions in these areas that will deliver an Airbnb-quality experience in pinpointing a counterparty and closing a contract. Over the next several years we should expect a big improvement, across a broad swathe of sectors, in our ability to pinpoint providers, contract with them, and schedule them. We will see new brand names other than Uber and Airbnb coming to the fore in each of these areas. The TxCs have already fallen, and the technology is not complex, we just need supplier and consumer behavior to catch up with the capability offered by the fallen TxC.

For example, why isn't there a service whereby I can book a plumber to fix my leaking faucet to arrive in 30 minutes and at a pre-agreed price (assuming the job is not more complex than I have intimated)? Why can't a pizzeria contract for a stand-in pizza-maker to show up within one hour if its head pizza maker calls in sick right before her shift?

CHAPTER 9

Makers of Products Need to Transform Them into Services

Nearly every new business model or service being launched into the market by an entrepreneur seems to feel the need to describe itself as being *on-demand*. To some extent, many of the services *are* somewhat on-demand—certainly compared to how non-demand things used to be. True on-demand is the right service at exactly the right time, with none of those pesky TxCs that get between me and my wants and turn me into a terrible two-year-old having a tantrum because my wants are not being immediately satisfied.

PRODUCT MAKERS ARE FOCUSED ON THE WRONG TYPE OF INNOVATION

My inventory dump exists as I need all these things to give me the illusion that I am getting a quasi on-demand service. If I want the hedge trimmed, I can go into my garage and pick up the hedge trimmer, recharge it, and away we go. Ownership is as close to on-demand as the world can offer now.

Given the importance of ownership as a safety blanket to customers, innovation and entrepreneurship in today's world of hedge trimming is framed in the wrong way. Go and talk to the makers of hedge trimmers, and no doubt they will be focused on performance dimensions such as making the trimmers lighter (trimming hedges for an hour or two will test the biceps), cheaper, and better cutting. All of these improvements are welcome, but this expenditure of energy on improving device performance misses the point. On most of these performance dimensions, the makers of things are often reaching diminishing returns. Hedge trimmers are already remarkably cheap and have probably been subject to limited product performance improvements over the past 20 years.

The designers and manufacturers of these things are barking up the wrong hedge. They probably haven't realized that I don't want a hedge trimmer—I want my hedge already trimmed. It's a big difference. I want it done in the lowest TxC, lowest hassle manner.

REFRAMING WANTS AND NEEDS— TURNING EVERYTHING FROM A PRODUCT TO A SERVICE

So, what is it that I want? From the microeconomists, sometimes one encounters the notion that utility derives not from things but from the characteristics of things. The thing itself doesn't matter; it is what the thing can do for us. "We gain satisfaction not from toothpaste as such but from 'decay prevention' and 'mouth-freshening' qualities which the toothpaste provides."[*]

Let's start with one of my important assets—my car. It sits on-demand like an ever-ready sentinel in my driveway (like my hedge trimmer in my garage) awaiting my call to action. You won't be surprised to hear me suggest that, sometime soon, some transportation service along the lines of an Uber or a shared usage offering from a car company might meet my wants well enough to persuade me to let go of ownership of the car. This is because I don't actually want a car; I want to get from A to B at a certain time in a timely, safe, clean, low-cost manner.

---

[*] Martin Ricketts, *The Economics of Business Enterprise*, 3rd ed. (United Kingdom: Edward Elgar Publishing 2002), 68.

We can reframe the "want" for all our assets similarly:

I don't want a hedge trimmer	I want my hedge trimmed
I don't want a ladder	I want to be able to reach up to something high, like upstairs windows and gutters
I don't want a bicycle	I want to get from specific point A to B faster than walking
I don't want a rice maker	I want cooked rice at 6:35 p.m.
I don't want a hairbrush	I want brushed hair

We have the (bad) habit of ownership and won't be quick to relinquish it for most of our possessions. Over time, as entrepreneurs bring forward propositions that allow us to consume the product as a service, we will come to realize that these things we own are merely means to an end—the end being the satisfaction of our specific want at that point in a perfect manner. For most items, we have no emotional attachment—ownership or rentership of them will become a cold-blooded calculus of relative TxCs.

Entrepreneurs are already deploying subtly different propositions (new ways to exchange) to nudge us along the early steps of the on-demand journey. For mundane items such as razors and razor blades, coffee, pet food, meal kits, and underwear, there are new ventures trying to get us to adopt subscription services—committed monthly or otherwise periodic purchases. While these subscription services are not quite on-demand, they give the feeling that we have "outsourced" the purchase decision and that we are starting to consume the goods as a service rather than a product.

Even those new ways to exchange will themselves be overtaken by even better ways to exchange, which will themselves again be overtaken by better ways to exchange and so forth. Each step along the way becomes progressively more on-demand. Remember: I don't want razors and blades—I want my stubble gone. The entrepreneur who figures out how to fulfill that want has a chance of winning.

WANTS ARE TRICKY TO PIN DOWN

Let's return to our want to get from point A to point B. While our want is stated as being to "get from A to B," unfortunately, it is not. Our want to get from A to B might in fact be "I want to meet my mates to watch the game" or "I want to attend a business meeting." Those are different wants altogether from "get from A to B." Even when we explore "attend a business meeting," the underlying want might be "to meet certain people." Even then, why do I want to meet them? It might be "to build trust." The reason for wanting to build trust might be "to negotiate a price for the goods that I want to buy."

Marketers will understand that we never completely satisfy people's wants. The true want (if such a thing exists) keeps receding to the horizon as the world gets better and better (from a TxC perspective) at satisfying immediate apparent wants. The need for entrepreneurship to anticipate and deliver against our evolving wants will always be with us.

ENVIRONMENTAL BENEFITS OF CONVERTING PRODUCTS INTO SERVICES

It may sound like we are heading toward a consumerist heaven in which individuals obsess over the satisfaction of their wants and where we end up in a frenzy of excessive consumption and completely trash the environment even further. Nothing could be further from the truth. Asset utilization in a low-TxC world should go through the roof. If I use my hedge trimmer 1 percent of the time (the reality is more like 0.1 percent or 0.01 percent of the time), then when minimizing the TxCs allows it to be exposed to the sharing economy, its utilization might go up by 100 times. The world will need only 1 percent or less of the hedge trimmers that are produced today.

TxCs are the epitome of waste. They are the costs that inhibit exchange. Eliminating them increases value in the world, even in the absence of more consumption. A world in which wants are met more precisely with less TxCs is a world in which there is far more efficient utilization of resources, and far less junk going to landfills.

TECHNIQUE F:
WEANING PEOPLE AND BUSINESSES OFF THEIR
OWNERSHIP FIXATION

At this stage, you are hopefully able to at least nod your head at the downsides of ownership—the sprawling dump of assets, the idleness of all these expensive (and cheap) items, the hassles of owning and caring for them, the inflexibility of having them on hand, the real and obscure costs of disposal. As TxCs decline and the imperative for ownership subsides, how might entrepreneurs take advantage?

STEP ONE: EXAMINE POSSESSIONS
TO SURFACE CANDIDATES
FOR NON-OWNERSHIP

Returning to the 300,000-odd items in my house, which ones are ideal to switch from an ownership to a rentership or sharing model? Clearly, with a score of 300,000 and little evidence yet of a mindset change, ownership is still winning the day hands down. Great news for the next generation of our entrepreneurs!

A great way to surface entrepreneurial opportunities is to walk around a house and list out the household assets. Start brainstorming one by one how these could be reimagined under a rentership or sharing model. In Chapter 12, we will review assets owned by companies, charities, and governments as they progressively open to the market.

The first place to start is high-value household assets, but unsurprisingly, this is where entrepreneurs are already working away:

- **Transportation (cars, bikes, scooters, etc.).** The impending shift from owned transportation to transport-on-demand has been well signposted and is covered in other parts of this book.
- **Accommodation.** It is likely that we are going to go through a secular shift from a model of high level of home permanency (owned or long-term rentals) to a

model of more flexible contracting for accommodation. The reality of the world we live in is one of more flexible and uncertain career paths, more migration, partial working from home, etc.

Certain segments might benefit from a flexible contracting service that serves them up places to stay based on where they need to be for work or pleasure in a particular season, or month, or week, or day. When we have relinquished many of our physical possessions (including our omnipresent hedge trimmer!) and are accessing lots of things as services on demand, then flexible contracting for accommodation becomes much simpler. An analogy for this might be office hot-desking, or allocating desks to workers as needed rather than each worker having an assigned desk. With all documents and applications in the cloud and accessible on-demand, a person's office is wherever they are.

- **Boats and other high value but infrequently used assets** are perfect prospects for sharing or rentership economy models given their low levels of utilization.
- **Tuxedos and women's formalwear.** Tuxedos have been shared for a long time, and rightly so, as they are an expensive and infrequently used item. When one only uses a tuxedo once every two or three years, it is remarkable how the suit seems to have shrunk in the meantime. Tuxedo rental companies have managed to get us over our TxC of worry about the cleanliness of the suit. If I am to spill some beer (or worse) on a suit, perhaps it is better if I impose those TxCs on someone else. Similarly, women's formalwear is a sector where new sharing economy players are making inroads.

There are objects or assets that may be of lower value and below the radar for entrepreneurs such as parking spaces in front of my house, sharing of first editions of books, rarely used kitchen appliances, and garden equipment and furniture.

There are items where it does not foreseeably make any sense to deliver them through a sharing or on-demand manner:

- My hairbrush
- The pen on my desk
- My jeans

Having reviewed lots of household items, hopefully at this point you have a list of owned things that you believe have the potential to be "un-owned."

STEP TWO: DEEP DIVE ON A POSSIBLE SHARING MODEL

Having built your list of possible items for non-ownership, now it is time to do a deep dive on whichever ones you see as most promising. We'll start with garden equipment. As far as I can tell, no one has built a globally scaled rentership or sharing economy business for it.

Every week or two in the summer, I need a lawnmower and some tools like a fork and spade. Maybe once or twice a year, I need an edger for the lawn, my trusty hedge trimmer, and a chainsaw. Every once in a blue moon, I need a long-reach hedge trimmer to get to those difficult-to-cut places and an extendable chainsaw for those very high branches that I want to lop off. And on even rarer occasions, I need one of the 60 or so other items of garden equipment that are available for hire from the nearest equipment rental company (about four miles from my house). These arcane devices include a post-hole digger for putting up a post, a pressure washer for the patio, a rototiller, a sledgehammer, a lawn aerator, etc. I am not exactly trying to recreate Kew Gardens in London, but there are times when the job I am trying to do cries out for one of these devices. Only once in my life have I visited the equipment hire company; in the meantime I have found some way to muddle through (or hired someone to do the work).

What should I do, given all these needs? I try to avoid buying equipment other than the pieces that I use a lot (lawnmower, fork, spade, etc.). The equipment hire option is too much like the Blockbuster experience and always turns out to be surprisingly expensive.

Yet almost every piece of garden equipment I could ever need (and probably dozens more) is sitting in a garden shed within a radius of 100 to 200 yards of where I am sitting right now. At the time that I need it, there is almost a 99 percent chance that it is sitting idle. The owner is probably not averse to lending it to a neighbor if it is guaranteed to be returned intact and clean. That owner probably also has some experience in the practicalities of using a post-hole digger that she is happy to impart.

But, as we discussed earlier in this book, the chances of such a neighborhood cooperative emerging by itself is extremely slim. We need an entrepreneur to come along with an offering to deal with all the TxCs inhibiting such local cooperative activity, which include the following aspects:

- A vetting system for members
- A way to regulate the ratio of "giving" versus "taking" by all members, to ensure people are acting as good citizens
- Maybe an Automobile Association–type breakdown repair for when equipment gets damaged or stops working
- A messaging capability
- Reviews and ratings to encourage neighborly behavior
- Some form of deposit or simple insurance
- A cleaning service
- Ratings and reviews
- Processes around pickup and drop-off or a delivery service

None of these aspects are rocket science. An entrepreneur should be able to minimize most of the TxCs. The question is whether enough of them can be crushed at this time to entice consumers to the new service. Maybe not now—maybe in the future. One very interesting aspect is that our entrepreneur does not need to know anything about gardening to start building a globally scalable gardening-focused business.

STEP THREE: DELIVER A WINNING PROPOSITION

There is a great deal of entrepreneurship going on in the world of transportation—ride offerings such as Uber or Lyft, ride-sharing among people heading to the same destination, and hourly rentals of bikes, scooters, and cars from distributed locations. Lots of other transportation business models will come to the fore over the coming years.

One business model in the area of transportation that bridges the gap between ownership and rentership offers the opportunity to sign up to one car company brand (e.g., Ford, Lexus, Mercedes), or one leasing company service, pay a monthly fee, and then have access to different cars depending on one's need at the time. For example, if I am heading to France on vacation with the family, I can "borrow" a minivan. If I am heading to the mountains for outdoor pursuits, I can get a 4X4. If am only moving around the city for the next month or two, I can get a small, easy-to-park car. If the weather is looking good for the next month, why not drive a convertible?

In effect, I can "de-average" my experience. Instead of being stuck with owning a vehicle that is optimized for one use, such as an around-town car that then means I am cramped while on vacation, I can have the right car, at the right time, for the right purpose. These sorts of services are only at the beginning of their lives.

The lesson from this is that to wean customers from their ownership fixation, an entrepreneur needs to conceive an irresistible rentership or sharing model. Simply offering a cheaper alternative to ownership is often not enough to change customer behavior. Someone might come up with a lawnmower rental service that costs less on a per-use basis than it would be for me to own the lawnmower, but if the TxCs of traveling to pick it up and hurrying to book it for the sunny afternoon are high, ownership will be preferable.

TxC FIVE:
REGULATION AND GOVERNMENT PROTECTION

Governmental regulation and protection exist to thwart or change the flow of exchange in ways that the government perceives as delivering social or political advantages. There are many ways in which this intervention happens:

- It inhibits, limits, or prohibits excess supply from meeting a source of demand. It might, for example, do this by banning imports (or imposing tariffs) from a particular country, perhaps with the goal of protecting the existing suppliers (and their workers).
- It imposes standards on certain sources of supply—e.g., no child labor, safety restrictions, which indirectly, or deliberately, inhibit or prohibit those suppliers from reaching the market in the government's jurisdiction.
- It subsidizes certain sources of supply or sources of demand. For example, it might decide to give tax breaks or grants to first-time home buyers.
- It allows certain groups to restrict access to their profession (accountants, vets, lawyers, optometrists) to ensure minimum quality standards in those professions.

Governments put these TxCs in place to achieve perceived social or political goals. The quid pro quo for pursuing these goals is that some exchanges that would add value to society are forgone. Since voluntary exchange should lead to better outcomes for both parties, governments need to know that the social and political benefits of their interventions (e.g., blocking imports of products in certain sectors) exceed the direct exchange value lost. This is an extremely difficult calculation to make.

However, these governmental interventions typically only have a limited half-life of effectiveness. The source of supply or demand that is inhibited by the intervention will inevitably look for avenues to reestablish exchange with the blocked counterparties—whether by redesigning its product or breaching the regulation (e.g., drug dealers).

CHAPTER 10

Why Are Transaction Costs Falling Rapidly?

Throughout the millennia, the most pressing TxCs that inhibited exchange have always been the most basic ones. Geography was a burden due to primitive modes of transportation, and trust between tribal groups is believed to have been pretty low. Money didn't exist as a means of exchange. Trade and exchange outside of local interpersonal exchange was almost nonexistent. Without trade and exchange, it is impossible to live anything but a subsistence life—a subsistence life being one where each group must meet all of its own needs without meaningful exchange, and therefore without economic value in group members' lives.

Thankfully, due to declines in TxCs and the consequent increase in the complexity of exchange in our world today, many of us live lives that are a long way from subsistence. Each of us has a microscopically narrow range of skills or assets, and we use those skills via the medium of money to exchange with others to meet our other wants and needs.

We covered the formula for "spinning straw into gold" by taking advantage of decreasing TxCs in Chapter 4. In Chapter 5, we reviewed the major categories of TxCs: an inability to search the market; lack of trust; the tyranny of geography; an inability to pinpoint a counterparty and close a contract; regulation and government protection; lack of certainty in payment/transfer of value; the opportunity cost of people's time; and monetary TxCs.

Falling Transaction Costs → Increased Exchange →
Opportunities for Entrepreneurs and Value for Everyone

But we haven't covered why TxCs are falling so rapidly right now. Why does it feel like we are going through an unprecedented era of entrepreneurship and new types of exchange?

FUNDAMENTAL INVENTIONS

The value creation taking place in the world through enhanced exchange is being shaped by the fundamental inventions that have been discovered or created in the recent past. These include:

- The internet
- GPS
- Mobile telephony
- Blockchain
- Ubiquitous software

What is unclear to many people is how these inventions make their way into national statistics (GDP, National Income, productivity). These fundamental inventions, in and of themselves, don't put food on the table or directly meet people's wants and needs. Just because some bright inventor in his or her garage invents GPS does not mean the world is a more valuable place. No value is created until exchange happens (except speculative value on stock markets, which anticipate expected consequential value in the real world). These inventions do not increase the productivity of farming a field of corn or increase the throughput in a steel mill—the effects of which would be straightforward to calculate. Indeed, economists often scratch their heads when they try to work out if and how all the investment in software over the past two or three decades is feeding into national productivity statistics.

HOW FUNDAMENTAL INVENTIONS DELIVER VALUE

Fundamental inventions lower TxCs. Many of the most profound inventions in recent decades act like wrecking balls pounding away at TxCs. Fundamental inventions don't yield value in and of themselves—they lower TxCs and through this mechanism open up new swathes of exchange and avenues for entrepreneurship.

Taking the internet as one invention, you can see how it impacts, dramatically, virtually all of the eight groupings of TxCs. The internet has revolutionized the ability to search for good exchange counterparties (e.g., better plumbers). It has introduced subtle new ways of spreading trust—through reviews and ratings and through new enterprises designed to inject trust into situations where no trust existed (take, for example, Uber, which acts as a trusted party between you and an army of entrepreneurial private drivers). The internet has been the biggest enemy of TxCs that the world has seen so far, but who knows what inventions will come next? We have been enjoying the value-creation fruits of the internet for the past two or three decades, and we are likely to be only in the foothills of its value creation potential.

The same is true for the other major inventions. The invention of the mobile phone did not directly add value to our lives. It did, however, attack TxCs and unleash exchange as a result. A trawler owner with fish to sell can search the market (using his phone) to find out if there is a higher-price buyer in the next town. I can order a ride on my phone and track the driver enroute, thus enhancing my trust in the exchange and minimizing the opportunity cost of my time.

So, a more accurate formula for spinning straw into gold would be:

Fundamental Inventions → Falling Transaction Costs →
Increased Exchange → Opportunities for
Entrepreneurs and Value for Everyone

o o o

While there are some prognosticators that fret about the opportunities for future economic growth, they will hopefully be proved wrong. Our inventors are busy creating fundamental inventions, and our entrepreneurs have only started on the journey of exploiting the lower TxCs open to them as a result of these fundamental inventions.

TxC SIX:
PAYMENT AND TRANSFER OF VALUE

It is hard to believe that at time of writing in 2023, it is still difficult to transfer money from person to person. Payments should be simple, but they aren't:

* I can use a service such as PayPal or Venmo, but maybe the counterparty is not a member. It takes several keystrokes to make the payment happen, especially the first time I need to send money to someone.
* I can pull some cash out of my pocket, but cash is insecure and dirty.
* I can organize a bank transfer, but passing routing and account numbers around does not engender confidence.
* Service X might work in China or the United States or France, but we seem to be a long way from a simple and ubiquitous money transfer service that works globally.
* Payment systems are often oligopolies, as any useful payments system must have many participants for it to be of use. Oligopolies are ideally positioned to charge well for the use of their services.
* The payment rail is separate from the physical or electronic delivery of the product or service. Delivery goes to the seller through a different channel, and the two rarely happen at the same time. The buyer pays in advance and suffers the worry that the product or service may not be up to expectations, or the supplier risks delivering first and worrying about subsequent payment.

Even though digitization is upon us, and payments should be highly prone to digitization, if my neighbor wants to borrow my hedge trimmer and pay me $5 for the privilege, he or she is still likely to pull a grubby five-dollar bill out of their pocket and pass it over to me.

Payments impose TxCs. Yes, the monetary charge for a transaction is a clear TxC, and surely, over the next 5 to 10 years, we will be well served with simple, costless (or low cost), globally applicable payment mechanisms. The marginal cost of these transactions is zero, and pricing should gravitate to that level over time. Payments should become as simple as an uptick or downtick in a global ledger, perhaps using blockchain or some similar technology.

But right now payment imposes many more TxCs than just the monetary cost, and we have thwarted exchange. I might like to buy some products from China or Vietnam for a new business I want to set up, but the payment hassles get in the way. This leaves gaps for entrepreneurs to solve the TxCs, or to offer some service that helps consumers and businesses to sidestep the TxCs.

CHAPTER 11

Why Transaction Costs Eliminate the Price Space Most of the Time

n Economics 101, we learned about supply and demand curves for products and services. "X" marked the spot where the supply and demand curves crossed, and this determined the price and quantity of the product to be exchanged. It was simple.

Txcs might have been touched on as something that one might need to consider in drawing the curves. But no one made it clear that TxCs destroy the potential for exchange almost 100 percent of the time. The true supply and demand curves rarely crossed, because the demand curves fell away down to the left and the supply curves moved up. Thwarted exchange is like the dog that never barked: it doesn't happen, so we never think about it. *Thwarted exchange happens when TxCs eliminate the price space.*

THE THEORETICAL PRICE SPACE IS OFTEN EXTREMELY FAVORABLE

Let's start by considering the two empty parking spaces in my driveway. While I don't live in a very high demand (or high value) zone for parking, I am close enough to the city that, on occasion, there may be some people who would like to use my parking spots.

Exchange of my parking spots should be possible. In the spirit of sharing and squeezing the most out of an asset, my parking spaces should be available to the market when I don't want to use them myself. In fact, if I were a rational economist, I would include myself like any other prospective paying user of the parking spaces, competing with all the other potential parking spot users. I should be both the lessor (maximizing my revenues) and the lessee, thereby getting the incentive system right by separating ownership from usage.

Since my parking spots are empty while I am at work, I might be willing to let someone use them for $5 each during the day—maybe a neighbor, maybe a local company, or the local hotel. On St. Patrick's Day when the city is jammed, maybe I can extract some nice surge pricing. On December 20, there may be someone sitting at home thinking that he would like to go shopping in the city, but he is worried that the city will have no free parking spaces. He might be willing to pay up to $20 or $40 for the use of one of my parking spots for the day. His alternative is to stay at home and shop outside the city or join the frustrated hordes scavenging for a parking spot in the city. With zero marginal cost to me for the parking spots, there is only upside.

Perfect: we have a willing lender at $5 and a willing borrower at $20—a price space of $15 (Figure 11.1). There is plenty of scope for a possible transaction. We could split the difference and go for $12.50. More likely, as is the case in most of economics where there are multiple possible lenders, the borrower will capture most of the value and I will have to be happy with my $5. Our supply and demand curves from Economics 101 suggest that the market should clear and exchange take place.

What you will notice is the latent potential value creation for each side of the transaction: both parties could walk away happy, just like my example of buying the painting from the street vendor in Chapter 4.

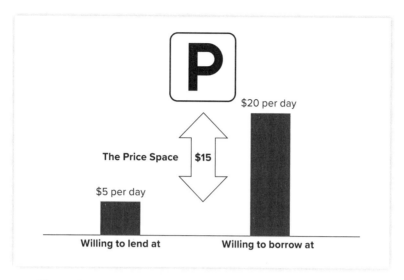

Figure 11.1 The Price Space for Making Transactions Happen

BUT TxCS EAT UP THE PRICE SPACE

Unfortunately, this transaction is unlikely to happen. The problem is all the TxCs for both the lender and the borrower.

I, as the lender, face TxCs along the following lines:

- Listing the parking spot on the web (In the old days I would advertise it in the neighborhood newsletter.)
- Keeping the listing up to date for the hours when I want to use it and not use it
- Finding the person to rent the spot
- Trusting the renter
- Figuring out some sort of insurance deal in case he or she backs into my pillar
- Having a lingering concern that my home insurance company won't like this arrangement one bit
- Tolerating a stranger coming and going in my front driveway
- Worrying that they will be late and won't be gone by the time I get home and need the spot
- Getting paid

- Suffering some passive-aggressive behavior from the local residents' association, which doesn't like this sort of thing
- Enduring some social embarrassment regarding being considered a cheapskate who is on the hunt for a measly $5

The borrower also faces TxCs:

- Deciding to search for a private parking spot (She may not even know such a service exists.)
- Discovering my parking spot
- Finding out if my spot is available for the exact hours that she wants it for
- Making some sort of contract with me
- Trusting that I am not going to be a pain to deal with
- Having some lingering concern about insurance and access rights
- Making a payment
- Worrying that she is not going to get back to the parking space before her allotted time is up

Interestingly, most of these TxCs could probably be overcome today if an able entrepreneur did a great job of pulling together a world-class service. No new technology would be required. This may be an example of a situation where TxCs have already fallen but entrepreneurs have yet to take advantage of the opportunity.

All these TxCs, and all we want to do is to let someone use a parking spot for $5. In fact, if it were a neighbor looking to use it, we would probably have been willing to give it to him or her for free. However, each of the nonfinancial TxCs is potent enough by itself to negate the exchange; it is simply not worth the hassle. Which is unfortunate as, despite goodwill on both sides, the failure to exchange means that both sides are out of pocket in a value sense, and the world is a tiny bit more inefficient and wasteful.

Hopefully you can appreciate that in a sufficiently low-TxC world, I would have to do absolutely nothing; the $5 would simply end up in my bank account and the parking spot would be used without me even noticing, or even being informed.

WHAT WE NEED IS SOMEONE TO CRUSH OUR TxC PROBLEMS

If you change the item in our example from my parking spots to a car or an empty apartment or a pizza, things start to get clearer. If we are Uber drivers and users, TxCs like these have been swiped out of the way. We can find each other seamlessly. We can contract with each other. We can set the time and place where we will meet, to the minute. We can pay each other. We can have a level of trust in each other as driver and passenger that was almost inconceivable barely a few years ago. Uber is a TxC-crushing machine—at some level, the corporate strategy for Uber is to relentlessly crush the TxCs that inhibit drivers and riders from exchanging.

If we are hosts or guests on Airbnb, we can also find each other. We can contract with each other. We can take advantage of all the types of service delivery improvements that Airbnb does to reduce TxCs between hosts and guests. We can pay each other. At some level it feels like Airbnb and other similar companies have developed a very long list of potential TxCs between hosts and guests and gone down through them one by one to reduce, mitigate, or eliminate them. While they might not use the language of economics, I would suspect something like this is exactly what they did. Uber, Airbnb, food delivery companies— they have all crushed the TxCs beyond the tipping point where the participants can take advantage of the positive price space (which has always existed but previously could not be accessed) and exchange in the market.

ONCE LOWER TxCS MAKE EXCHANGE WORTHWHILE, HUGE MARKETS OPEN

No doubt there are players on the internet in the short-term private parking platform business. They just haven't crushed the TxCs enough yet to create a deep, wide, liquid market. But when and if the TxCs get lowered enough, there is a chance such a business (and hundreds or thousands of other home parking type businesses) could go from not making sense at all to making complete sense, almost overnight. If a tipping point in TxCs for private parking is reached, private parking could go from a business in which only a tiny quantity of exchange takes place (such as in the city center or beside a stadium) to one with a vast quantity of exchange.

Many people believe that all these rentership and sharing economy opportunities are quite small—capturing small pebbles of value ($5 for a parking spot) and yielding only small entrepreneurial opportunities, with minor price arbitrages along the lines suggested by Israel Kirzner, one of the great thinkers on the subject of entrepreneurial opportunity.* This is wrong. The new total value pools have the potential to be very large as these are not gardening or parking space businesses; these are software platforms that exist in the cloud.

As it would be a software platform in the cloud, the short-term private parking platform provider has the chance of becoming a national or global business. It is not in the parking business—it is in the TxC-crushing business. In a modestly sized city like Dublin with roughly 500,000 private households, most of which would have a parking spot, a good platform operator could possibly open up a market of hundreds of thousands of spots, never mind weekend spots in places like office parks. Each of these spots could have value. Consider the loss of value by the unfortunate nonoccurrence of the parking spot transaction. Yes, there was a price space of $15 for the use of the spot for the day. But there was also the destruction of value suffered by the prospective parking spot renter who lost the pleasure and benefits of a day's Christmas shopping or got in their car and circled the city for a long time waiting for someone to leave a spot. There are a billion parking spots in the United States—four for each car. But perhaps only 5 percent of them are directly available to the market on a continuous basis.

These factors explain part of why companies like Uber and Airbnb have enormous market capitalizations. Again, consider the world before Uber and Airbnb; if someone had suggested that

---

* Israel Kirzner, *Competition and Entrepreneurship* (Chicago: University of Chicago Press, 2013), 81.

businesses of their scale could be built on the back of the humble taxi or vacation rental business, the proposals would have been laughable.

There are idle assets hiding in plain sight. Almost no one thinks about the revenue potential in their parking spots when they are buying a house today, but maybe they will in the future.

TxC SEVEN:
REDUCING THE OPPORTUNITY COST OF PEOPLE'S TIME

My time is valuable to me. It is especially valuable Monday through Friday during normal working hours. On Saturdays and Sundays and during evenings, it is less valuable. On Monday, Tuesday, and Wednesday evenings it is a lot less valuable.

So the TxC of wasted time during my valuable hours means that anyone who wants to exchange with me during those hours is going to struggle if the exchange requires my time. Popping out from work to go to the dentist or get my hair cut during a weekday, or to see a physiotherapist or open my front door to a plumber, is incredibly inconvenient and costly in a TxC sense.

Unfortunately, people who provide personal and household services seem determined to impose these costs on me and inhibit exchange. They try to impose their business model (which assumes that my time is valueless) on me. They want me to show up Monday to Friday during working hours. Surely in a world with both partners typically working, smart entrepreneurs should be looking at arbitraging between the value of the time of the person receiving the service and that of the person delivering the service. Why can't a plumber come at 9 or 10 p.m.? Why isn't the barber open until 10 p.m.? Gyms have figured this out.

Employers are starting to recognize this arbitrage. They often are the ones bearing the cost of this lost time. If a worker has a dental or medical appointment, that might entail the loss of a whole afternoon, given travel time.

Smart employers increasingly offer food and recreation to keep their employees fully productive on the premises rather than "wasting" time on less valuable activities. Some are being ambitious in offering other services. Could it make sense for employers to offer onsite services delivered by third parties for:

- Dental checkup (Fifteen minutes in the chair on premises results in little loss of work time)
- Medical checkup
- Haircuts
- Basic groceries
- Physiotherapist or chiropractor

TECHNIQUE G:
SLICING AND DICING PROPERTY RIGHTS

The process of exchange has an internal motor that drives it to become more complex over time as entrepreneurs hunt for value. More complexity means that the wants of customers can be met more precisely over time.

Increased complexity normally bumps up against TxCs. For example, if a local car dealer decides she wants to rent her excess cars out to people, it is far simpler to decide to rent the car in weekly blocks rather than hour by hour. The hourly approach might yield more gross revenue, but the higher TxCs (car cleaning, management time, customer service costs) would likely outweigh the higher revenue.

There are sectors that have embraced complexity and the consequentially higher TxCs. People used to rent out their properties for 6 or 12 months, until they discovered that Airbnb can could handle the complexity of short-term rentals. Even with Airbnb, the average stay is roughly six nights.* Perhaps over time the TxCs of handling a booking (checking guests in and out, cleaning, etc.) will be removed to the point where renting out an apartment can be profitable if it is let day by day to different people. If TxCs could be reduced even further, the apartment could be let just for the morning, afternoon, evening, or overnight. Maybe it could even be let hour by hour for meetings. Lower TxCs opens more compelling business propositions previously considered impossible. In technique G we will examine how progressive complexity, by slicing and dicing the property rights associated with the underlying asset, is now easier to manage and can yield new business propositions.

---

* Airbnb website, 2022, https://blog.atairbnb.com/economic-impact-airbnb/.

COMPLEX EXCHANGE IN THE WORLD OF CAPITAL MARKETS

The finance industry is home to probably the most complex exchanges in the world. The world of finance takes an asset—which could be a power plant, a company, a patent, a forest, royalties from music—and figures out how to slice and dice the ownership rights (the right to different cash flows) from that asset. These rights to the different cash flow streams from the asset are then sold to different investors.

Different types of assets can have their cash flows sliced in different ways:

- **Mortgages:** The cash flows from a bundled set of mortgages can be disaggregated to meet the cash flow and risk requirements of different investors.
- **Power plants:** Different types of investors will be interested in the senior debt, the subordinated debt, and the equity cash flows.
- **Early-stage tech companies:** Different investors at different stages of the growth of the firm (seed, Series A, growth, etc.) have different claims, via different types of preferred and ordinary shares and loans, on the cash flows from the sale or initial public offering of the company.

This slicing creates economic value as different investors have their specific wants met in a more perfect manner than previously. The inbuilt dynamic for entrepreneurs (investment bankers in this case) is to pursue more and more complexity over time. TxCs such as legal contracts and payments to intermediaries act as a brake on this complexity. As TxCs fall and a higher level of complexity become manageable, the type of activity we see in capital markets will spread to all sectors, including lower value assets owned by individuals.

o o o

One exciting avenue for brainstorming new propositions is to take the approach of finer-grained slicing and dicing of ownership and usage rights and apply it to all sorts of assets. Let's start with my driveway (but we could easily do this with any asset I might own).

MAXIMIZING DRIVEWAY SPACE AS AN INCOME-EARNING ASSET

My primary asset is my house. Yes, I am the owner of the house, but I could decide to rent out the house, thereby granting some rights to the tenant, while I remain as the residual owner. If that tenant is a student and only needs the property for the nine months of the school year, I could decide to become a host for Airbnb during the summer when demand is highest, thereby granting temporary rights to my guests. For the two weeks at Christmas and two weeks at Easter when the student is gone, I could also offer the property for rent. You can start to see how progressively finer slicing and dicing of the usage of the asset can maximize my revenue, assuming the coordination costs are not overwhelming.

Thankfully, there are people like rental agents and Airbnb who can take care of the TxCs on my behalf (particularly the contracting TxCs). Slicing and dicing further, I could decide to rent out my two relatively idle parking spots. There are lots of potential use cases:

* Annual open-ended renting of the spots to local businesses who need parking spots for their staff or their clients
* Extremely short-term renting for times when all the parking spaces on my street are full
* Evening parking for people going to restaurants
* Weekly parking for the weeks when I am on vacation
* Daily parking for when I am traveling for work
* Overflow parking for the nearby hotel for big events like weddings
* Parking for parents dropping off and picking up from school

In the same way that we can all understand why a landlord can probably make more money being a short-term host on Airbnb rather than getting locked into a long-term lease, the more the "property rights" over the parking space can be disaggregated, the more potential value I can capture. These rights can be disaggregated repeatedly to lower levels, all the time increasing value—it is not necessarily the case that one reaches diminishing returns over time.

The TxCs for me today to manage some sort of disaggregated use of my parking spaces are prohibitive. As we discussed in the previous section, there isn't even a broad-based effective marketplace for medium-term rental of private parking spaces. But in the future, TxCs are going to be crushed by some third party, and hopefully I will have to do nothing as the fees for the disaggregated rights to my parking spots accumulate in my bank account.

Next, let's look at rental of commercial offices.

FLEXIBLE CONTRACTING FOR COMMERCIAL OFFICE SPACE

In the post-Covid world, companies are trying to figure out how to balance working from home and working from the office. The challenge is the disconnect between what companies and their staff want and what is on offer.

Companies might want a disaggregated set of services such as:

- Access to an office only on Tuesdays and Fridays (but not on Mondays, Wednesdays, and Thursdays)
- A small number of hot-desks that can scale up and down in number
- Monthly full staff get-togethers, but with the facility to hold smaller team meetings once or twice a week
- Occasional conference room access
- Access on demand to shared services for printing, copying, and other administrative activities

* A core permanent office with adjacent flexible space into which the company can scale up as needed
* Part-time support staff for designated occasional hours

The problem for companies is that landlords typically want full-time, long-term leases with guaranteed rental income. On the other extreme of the spectrum, there are very flexible working situations such as WeWork and serviced offices from companies like Regus, which are comparatively expensive.

This ignores the 95 to 99 percent of the market where companies are already locked into long-term leases. They know they are not utilizing their space to the maximum. They might want to disaggregate some of their rights by offering access to conference rooms, use of a staffed reception desk, flexible access to some office space with desks, Wi-Fi, etc.

To date, this type of arrangement has historically been problematic—leases might not allow it, companies might not have a very clear view on their own needs, managing security issues may be challenging, and so on. But the primary barrier is that companies in long term leases generally do not consider themselves to have an asset that can be leveraged—in the same way that people with parking spaces rarely consider them to be monetizable assets. The TxCs of finding matching prospective lessees with highly specific needs, constructing more complex multitenant leases, and managing the coming and going of staff of different companies is only starting to be possible.

○ ○ ○

In technique G, we have shown how entrepreneurs should look at every asset in the world (small or large) and consider how the rights to those assets could be sliced and diced with those disaggregated rights being transferred to the party that would value them most. Lower TxCs will make this process possible. There must be some investment bank out there that would like to securitize the 10-year cash flows from the disaggregated property rights to the two parking spots in front of my house and pay me an up-front lump sum. $30,000 anyone? $25,000?

CHAPTER 12

The Trifecta of Accelerators: the Internet of Things, Idle Assets, and Marginal Cost Pricing

TxCs are falling on fertile ground. Right now, there are three accelerators working together that are turbocharging the impact of falling TxCs:

1. **The Internet of Things.** The world's assets have largely been stranded and stuck in an "off" position in relation to the market. The Internet of Things is about to turn them "on."

2. **Idle assets.** The world's physical assets are grossly underutilized, due in large part to many being stuck in single-use mode (for their owners). Higher utilization of these assets will perhaps be the biggest value opportunity the world has ever seen.

3. **Marginal cost pricing.** The price of all these existing assets has already been paid. Increased utilization will likely come at a very low marginal cost.

These three accelerators are reinforcing each other and laying the path for fast exploitation of opportunities.

1. THE INTERNET OF THINGS: TURNING THE ASSETS OF THE WORLD ON

If wave one of the internet was getting most of the people in the world online, wave two is going to bring the assets of the world online. This will be via the Internet of Things (IoT) and its successors. IoT refers to an asset that can be accessed, monitored, and driven remotely through a network, thus having the potential to *turn it on* to the market. If the asset is an electricity generator in a village, in an IoT world an engineer or the generator's owner can dial in remotely to perform diagnostics on the generator, set the times for it turning on and off, offer the power generated to local people and businesses for a time-of-day price, and more importantly from our perspective, grant an entrepreneur access to it.

While the IoT has many positive benefits for the owner of the assets, in terms of managing and optimizing use of their assets, the IoT has the far more interesting potential to transform the economic value of these assets by exposing them to the market. The end point on the horizon is that every asset in the world could be connected online, with a notional green and red traffic light system regarding when it will be available for use by its owner, or for "renting" by a third party. The software infrastructure will be in place to allow entrepreneurs to access and drive these assets.

There are a lot of things in the world. With 300,000-odd things in my house, I don't need to speculate about the size of the "things" market globally. It is plenty big; it is everything.

One reason to be so enthusiastic about the short- to medium-term prospects for entrepreneurship in the world is that (virtually) all these assets are about to move from the category of being stranded solely for their owner's use, into the category of active participant in the global economy. These assets will go from being stranded and inaccessible to accessible and rentable overnight, assuming the owner is willing to open access; if the third party is able to use the assets in a way that involves zero TxCs for the owner, why wouldn't the owner want to capture some value?

Turning My Things On

We will look at corporate assets and non-personal assets in the next section. First, however, it is fun to consider what might happen if I turned my assets on to the market. Consider the following:

- **My parking spot:** If I put an internet-enabled sensor on my parking spot, it becomes *searchable* by people hunting for a parking spot. My parking spot becomes a node in an interconnected web.
- **My fridge:** My fridge will know that I need milk and will order it. But might some entrepreneurs come up with a business proposition for all the half-empty refrigerators and freezers? That's a lot of "free," distributed, chilled space.
- **My toothbrush:** Maybe there will be benefits to tracking the way that I brush my teeth—up and down or left to right—to get me to adopt best brushing techniques over time. The side benefit will be that the toothbrush is now available to an entrepreneur to figure out what to do with my brush during its downtime. I dread to think what that use might be.
- **My books:** Maybe if all the books in my house (as well as those of my neighbors) were to be IoT-enabled, some budding entrepreneur could create a neighborhood library (with real books rather than e-books) whereby neighbors pass books to each other).

Currently, IoT units and software cost money and would be cost-prohibitive for these uses. Eventually, however, the cost of the units and software will trend toward zero.

2. IDLE ASSETS: THE WORLD'S ASSETS ARE ONLY USED TO A TINY PERCENTAGE OF THEIR POTENTIAL

By some estimates, the total value of the physical assets in the world is $360 trillion. Only when you look closely at these assets do you realize that they are remarkably underutilized.

Underutilized assets, valued at trillions of dollars, are potentially about to be turned "on" to the market. Could there possibly be an opportunity for entrepreneurs here?

We live in a just-in-case world. Everything in our homes is there just in case we might think about using it. Even the things we do use somewhat regularly are only used to a tiny fraction of their potential. For most of the time these assets are idle, locked into indolence by TxCs, and can't be exposed to third parties who might want to use them. No one can search the market and find out that these assets are idle and available to be used. The possible counterparties are not used to dealing with each other and probably lack mutual trust. Contracting for the use of the assets is challenging. Physical access to them is almost impossible. Payment is a pain. There is a plethora of other concerns such as insurance, last mile delivery of the assets back and forth, the opportunity cost of people's time, etc. In short, these assets are normally only available to their owner when their owner has need for them. The rest of the time they are idle. The same is true for corporate assets. As TxCs fall, these just-in-case assets will be transformed into just-in-time assets and release the value currently wasted through underutilization.

Types of Assets

At this point, you might be saying to yourself that, yes, we all have some idle assets, but isn't it all a bit marginal? It's a bicycle that goes unrepaired and unused in a garage, or our ubiquitous hedge trimmer that barely gets an outing more than once or twice per year. Maybe it's a paper clip that lies in my office drawer. Who can be bothered chasing pennies and five-dollar bills? Is the sharing economy just for twentysomethings who can't rub two quarters together and are happy to camp on someone's couch? Is the aspirational prize of higher or even full utilization of the world's assets truly worth pursuing?

The answer is yes. We just can't see the waste (and the consequential opportunity) as it is obscured behind impenetrable TxCs. Which categories of assets are we talking about?

- **Household assets.** These include houses, apartments, cars, clothes, bikes, paper clips, toothbrushes, parking spots—you name it.
- **Company assets.** These could include offices, warehouses, equipment, software systems, vehicles, the time of staff, intellectual property, legal skills, and cash. While some companies have a focus on 24/7 utilization of factories and distribution centers, most offices are customarily used for only 8 to 10 hours Monday through Friday.
- **Governmental assets.** These include parks, facilities, roads, rivers, buildings, legions of bureaucrats, random real estate plots, offices used for only eight hours per day, and power stations.
- **Skills.** Perhaps the most underutilized asset in the world is the excess supply of labor, which is unfortunately in the wrong place (or not discoverable at the point of need) to meet the excess demand elsewhere. This could be our house painter who is just too far away, or it could be the nearby plumber in whom I don't have sufficient trust to contract him for the work.
- **Intangible assets.** These include the empty car spaces in front of my house and the patent I filed that could be used by company X, if only they knew about it.

In summary, idle assets may include all the assets of the world. If, as becomes apparent on close review, all the assets in the world are grossly underutilized, there will be plenty of value to keep generations of entrepreneurs occupied. Not to state the obvious, but if an asset is only being used for less than 10 percent of its capacity, then its usage can potentially be boosted tenfold. It is likely that the value pools from higher utilization of the world's assets could be the greatest entrepreneurial opportunity. Everything in the world will be up to be "Airbnb-ed."

3. MARGINAL COST ECONOMICS ARE EXTREMELY HARD TO COMPETE AGAINST

What Are Average Cost Economics?

Let's return to our hedge trimmer example. I could decide to set up a business renting out hedge trimmers and work on crushing the TxCs for borrowers. To get the business going, I buy a bunch of hedge trimmers and put ads on the internet. Hopefully customers will book hedge trimmers online and come and pick them up (or preferably I offer delivery).

The challenge with this business model is that I need to charge borrowers enough to cover the *average* cost of a hedge trimmer. For example, if the hedge trimmer costs $200 and is good for 50 intensive uses before it starts needing repairs or replacement or a deep cleaning, then about $4 of cost needs to be absorbed in the fee to each borrower. I also need to amortize the cost of my business premises across each of the rentals. I need insurance for the premises and for the hedge trimmers. My salary and the full labor costs of my staff need to be added into the mix. All these costs must be averaged into the price that I charge the borrowers of the device before I turn a dollar of profit.

What Are Marginal Cost Economics?

Contrast this to the homeowner who is content to lend out her hedge trimmer. She already owns the trimmer, so she views it as "free" and doesn't need to amortize the cost of it across the people who want to borrow it. She doesn't need to pay for a premises to store it—the garage has lots of space. The insurance cost is buried in her home policy. She might consider the opportunity cost of her time as free, especially on the weekend—in fact, she may enjoy the process of getting to know her neighbors.

Her monetary marginal cost is almost zero, although of course there are hassles and TxCs that will need to be taken into consideration. Assuming some TxC-crushing company has done all the heavy lifting to eliminate the hassles for her and the borrower, then she may be willing to lend the device for, say, $5.

This is because she only has to think about her marginal costs—all the rest of the costs are sunk and gone. Virtually everything she charges falls to the bottom line as a profit. The homeowner as the supplier of a hedge trimmer (as opposed to the person attempting to build a dedicated hedge trimmer lending business) is thus very hard to compete against—players with marginal cost economics have a major advantage over players that need to cover their average costs.

Consider the example of the gig driver—he probably owns his car, which is sitting idle for much of the time, and he is already absorbing the monthly depreciation. He can pick working hours when the opportunity cost of his time is particularly low. Becoming a gig driver means that there are higher fuel costs and more wear and tear than if he wasn't doing the gig driving. He probably should be paying incremental insurance. The gross fares earned minus the cost of gas becomes income to the driver. His marginal costs are very low, and if he wanted to, he could still make a good profit per hour even by charging low prices. Compare this to the regulated taxi driver: she needs to amortize the cost of vehicle, the cost of the license, and probably a high insurance cost over the total number of rides she gives before she starts to earn any incremental income.

The driver with the marginal cost economics has a huge advantage. These marginal cost economics are not just pertinent to the underutilized assets in people's home—they apply to almost every single asset in the world.

Dynamic Pricing to Optimize Net Profits

Most businesses have fixed pricing. My barber has a fixed price, except for a slightly lower rate for seniors on Tuesday morning. As previously discussed, the opportunity cost of my time might be a lot higher (or lower) than the opportunity cost of the time of my barber's other customers, or of my barber himself. Flexible pricing can increase exchange as it widens the price space for certain exchange that can absorb wasteful TxCs. My barber might be willing to stay open late on Thursday night for special customers who are willing to pay $30 for a haircut, as opposed to the $20 he regularly charges.

Dynamic pricing can expose new exchange and new business models. That extra amount might even make the barber willing to come to my home at a designated time. There are long-standing businesses that have dynamic pricing at their core—airlines, hotels, car rental, etc. These are highly seasonal businesses with high demand variability. Players in these sectors that are not smart at pricing do not last long.

Dynamic pricing is starting to seep into many new sectors of the economy. Airbnb hosts can charge what they want for different weeks. Given marginal cost economics, the hosts can flex prices low at times of low demand when there is competition from other hosts, or they can decide to withdraw their property from the market, maybe even to use it themselves. Indeed, the host might only advertise the property on Airbnb right at the top of the market each year when "surge" pricing is available, as only then is there a large enough price space to justify the TxCs of rental (e.g., if the owner needs to move out). One interesting analysis of Airbnb might be to understand the distribution of profit by rental across a year. Is a large percentage of the net profit (after accounting for direct costs and opportunity costs) attributable to a small number of weeks during the year? Is all the profit made in a tiny number of weekly rentals?

It is hard for traditional businesses to migrate to dynamic pricing as their customers are accustomed to fixed, predictable pricing. The new sharing and rentership economies have more leeway to introduce dynamic pricing. Using average pricing and average cost economics, there might never be positive price space for an exchange after absorbing TxCs. But with marginal cost economics and dynamic pricing, periodic instances of positive price space might emerge for the entrepreneur to exploit. For example, I might not offer my parking spaces when the price space is $10 or less (based on marginal cost economics), but if it is $20 or more, then the "green light" might come on and make my spot available to be searched for through the market.

DANGER FROM THE TRIFECTA OF IOT, IDLE ASSETS, AND MARGINAL COST ECONOMICS

As the world's assets (including the skills and time of all the workers) become available to the market in a traffic light (green or red) manner and stop being assets that are "stranded" because of TxCs, there is going to be vast capacity coming on-stream across asset and labor markets. All the excess supply, currently blocked from the market by TxCs, will need to be absorbed. The existing owners may be willing to accept very low marginal revenue.

The makers of hedge trimmers will suffer if my one hedge trimmer becomes the hedge trimmer of choice for 100 of my neighbors. As China opened up to the global economy in recent decades and its previously stranded excess labor capacity (due largely to protectionist TxCs) became available, economic activity shifted to China and other countries' manufacturing bases declined during a long period of global deflation as that excess supply began to be absorbed. One outcome of this trifecta might be extreme deflation in the price of assets and certain labor as these idle assets and excess skills are brought to the market.

TxC EIGHT:
MONETARY TxCS

When thinking about TxCs (to the extent anyone ever does!), people instinctively zone in on pesky, persistent monetary ones. Nobody likes those brokers fees, service charges, buy-sell margins, call-out charges, and middlemen margins.

However, for all the attention that they get, these costs are overrated as inhibitors of exchange. When probing into the behavior of consumers and businesses and examining why they do or don't undertake a specific exchange, one comes back time and again to the other seven categories of TxCs (the hassles) outlined in Chapter 5. This is good news for the entrepreneur—new business models are likely to arise from designing a reduced TxC offering in these areas, rather than by embarking on the diminishing returns footslog of reengineering processes to deliver lower costs and consequently lower monetary charges.

That said, monetary TxCs have long been an annoying feature of many markets. Since many transactions are simply bits and bytes flying between computers, the variable cost of executing many transactions does not even register on the negligibility scale. Most current monetary TxCs do not exist because there is a variable cost to be recouped through the fee; most exist because of some form of monopolistic or oligopolistic behavior whereby someone in the middle can impose a "tax" on the transaction. The internet is now eliminating many of these intermediation charges.

One example is online stock trading. Witness the relentless and inevitable decline of online trading charges toward zero. As systems became most efficient, the only thing preventing a reduction in costs to consumers was the determination of the existing providers to protect their revenue streams. But, inevitably, given the wide numbers of potential providers, the incentive for an individual player (especially newcomers) to break ranks on customer pricing was too great. As charges fell, the increase in quantities of shares traded increased vastly. Lower TxCs create new markets and vastly increase the volumes in existing ones.

Another notable example is Amazon Prime. This "free" delivery service (for an annual or monthly fee) is almost like a reverse TxC. One pays a fee to avoid fees. Clearly, it does cost something to have a package come from Amazon's facility to one's home or office, but Amazon has decided that the elimination of a variable cost (thereby wiping this TxC from the mind of the consumer) will multiply purchases and make the "free" delivery more than economically worthwhile.

Virtually all monetary TxCs have been falling; the good news for everyone (other than the existing intermediaries) is that we are about to head into a period of rapid decline in monetary TxCs as technologies such as blockchain become widespread. The pace of implementation of blockchain (and whatever successors or alternatives to blockchain emerge) might be unclear, but the final destination is not.

TECHNIQUE H:
FERRETING OUT IDLE ASSETS

Idle Assets = Potential Opportunities

In technique H we'll take a string of assets and explore the extent to which they are underutilized and why they might be underutilized.

Empty Housing

A good place to start is at the very top of the pyramid with people's most valuable item of all (in most cases)—the home itself. I'll use the stats from Ireland as I am most familiar with them.

Ireland has roughly 2 million homes (Irish census 2016*), of which 85.2 percent (1.7 million) are occupied, 9.1 percent (183,000) are vacant, 2.5 percent (50,000) have owners who are temporarily absent, and 3.1 percent (62,000) are holiday homes. Yet we have a dire homelessness problem whereby about 8,000 people are unhoused (perhaps 5,000 or fewer households) and suffer the indignity of not having somewhere to call home. No doubt, homelessness is a multifaceted problem involving mental health, job security, housing shortages, and bad fortune, and is tangled up in overlapping public policy objectives, but we have dire need on one side (excess demand) and vast quantities of idle inventory on the other (excess supply).

Separately, but closely related, we have a housing affordability problem due to an imbalance of supply and demand—the rate of household growth in Ireland is roughly 30,000 per annum and housing completions are 20,000 per annum. We know that TxCs are what prevent excess demand from being quenched by excess supply. Some social entrepreneur should be having a field day. We have plenty of houses. We must have a TxC problem.

Sticking with the homelessness problem rather than the affordability one, the owners of these idle assets must be facing certain TxCs that are inhibiting them from entering into an exchange with the unhoused. A proper forensic analysis is

---

* Central Statistics Office, Ireland, *Housing Report*, 2016.

required, but the owners of these assets may consider they face TxCs such as:

- The worry that if they put a tenant into a house for a short period of time they won't be able to remove the previously homeless tenant at the end of the lease
- A trust concern that the property will not be well looked after
- The hassle of going through a renting process
- A potential rental income that is immaterial to the potentially well-off owner of the property
- A worry about enforcement of landlord's rights if the landlord needs the property back for some other purpose

While one might debate whether these are inappropriate concerns on the part of the landlords, the fact remains that if the TxCs remain high in the minds of the landlords, by hook or by crook, the assets simply won't be put forward for exchange. We also run into the countervailing problem that the government has a desire to improve tenants' rights vis-à-vis landlords, thereby driving up landlords' TxCs and, unintentionally, wiping out the price space for exchange.

If we reframe the problem as a TxC problem rather than a social policy one, maybe new solutions can be brought forth. Maybe these TxCs can be reduced. For example, let's take the prospective landlord's concern that the property might not be looked after well—a concern that landlords have for all properties. Could someone (perhaps the government or the unhoused person or a charity or wealthy foundation) provide a guarantee or deposit to the landlord to inject trust? Maybe an insurance company could create a new type of contract to address these situations that is underwritten by one of the parties just mentioned? Maybe the prior rental history of the homeless person could be cataloged (e.g., via blockchain) as a way of enhancing reputation and building trust?

We need to put on our TxC glasses and do what Airbnb and other companies do—minimize as many TxCs as possible—to take advantage of the price space. These properties are empty, and so the marginal cost of renting them out should be very low absent the TxCs.

Homeowners rent to millions of complete strangers through Airbnb and other platforms using online ratings and reviews to garner trust. We should be able to figure out something for 8,000 of our citizens, given all the idle inventory of dwellings. With an average house price of about €270,000 (much higher in metro areas) and 15 percent of our 2 million homes completely unoccupied (as opposed to underutilized), that is an underutilized asset of €80 billion just in Ireland (population of 1.1 percent of the European Union). That's definitely a large enough addressable market for any of our budding entrepreneurs!

Empty Space in Houses

Our most valuable assets are often the most underutilized. Airbnb allows a person to capitalize on an otherwise idle real estate asset. A person might decide that he can rent out his home for a few months of the year (in peak season with lots of tourists around) and earn additional income from an asset where he is only incurring low marginal costs.

But Airbnb is only scratching the surface on tapping into idle home assets. One could sit around all day thinking up new ways to boost the utilization of this most valuable of assets:

* Renting a home out as a once-off while we are away on vacation
* Never letting a couch remain "unsurfed"
* Allowing access to our kitchen while we are out (or maybe in) for a few hours a day
* Letting someone use our new kitchen and dining room to host a dinner party
* Never having an unused bedroom in the house
* Offering use of a bathroom to someone in need (Who among us hasn't had a child with an urgent bathroom need? Or even worse, for ourselves—a time when willingness to pay might be extremely high!)
* Providing space in an attic for storage of idle assets of neighbors or others

- If we have a safe in our house, offering it as a safety deposit box for neighbors on vacation
- Putting up solar panels (or allowing someone to put up solar panels) on a roof
- Renting out a living room as a meeting space for local businesses as an alternative to a sterile hotel room
- Offering a parking spot in front of a house
- Allowing use of a home office setup for someone who needs a very temporary office

I can hear the "yes, buts" getting dialed up. As TxCs currently stand, these "yes buts" are completely legitimate. There are search, trust, access, payment, and awkward dealings TxCs involved in all these situations—and some are onerous, given how preciously we guard our personal spaces. But, if a third party comes along and crushes these TxCs for us in very simple ways—preferably so we don't even notice that our asset is being utilized—and giving us the chance to knock off a few mortgage payments per year, the equation comes back into balance.

My Labor and My Brain

The ability to plug my labor into a global on-demand network increased enormously in March 2020 with the arrival of Covid-19. To be more precise, the willingness to reconceive plugging one's labor into an on-demand network increased enormously, as the technology for collaboration and working online long predated 2020. As we discussed earlier, some of the best entrepreneurial opportunities are those that take advantage of TxCs that have long since fallen but that no other entrepreneur has pursued.

This global on-demand network means that, in many cases, we no longer need to waste time going into offices. Depending on our jobs—if we like waking at 5 a.m. and are happy to work until 8 a.m. when the rest of the family wakes up, then we can. Parents with children can commit to unusual hours (e.g., 7–11 p.m. each night). In summary, we can be far more efficient in deploying our labor and achieve a higher utilization of our time, if that is what we want. There is now more openness to employing people from other parts of the world.

The tyranny of geography just lightened a lot. Flexibility cre ates new possibilities for improving the utilization of labor.

Paper Clips

What about the lowest value items in our homes, such as the humble paper clip? While I am happy to have an inventory of paper clips on hand given their tiny cost, I am pretty sure that an exchange with my neighbors might make sense if they suddenly need paper clips on a Sunday afternoon for a report to be delivered first thing on Monday. My side of the exchange might be the satisfaction associated with being a good neighbor, and their side of the exchange might be a willingness to reciprocate at some stage down the road. The world becomes a happier, more valuable place. The paper clip that lay in my desk for 20 years with zero utilization is finally playing a role in the global happiness system.

Inventory in Businesses

One area where the true cost of idle assets is understood widely and where there is a strong focus on avoiding idle assets is in business inventory. Inventory is now a dirty word in the world of business.

Long gone are the days when companies would pile inventory at critical bottleneck points in a factory "just in case" they needed it. Whether is called Just-in-Time or the Toyota Production System or just plain shelf management in your local supermarket, most businesses understand the value of minimizing inventory. Any CFO or operations manager who is not keeping a close eye on inventory will find herself answering questions she would prefer not to answer. Inventory leads to waste, theft, working capital problems, and a wholly wrong ethic for running a state-of-the-art production facility.

That's not the way it used to be. When Japanese production and inventory philosophies came into the consciousness of US corporations in the 1970s and 1980s, they were largely dismissed—until more reliable, cheaper Japanese cars started showing up in US driveways. The change was not long in coming:

inventory in the corporate world is now hunted down assiduously and eliminated.

MANY ASSETS HAVE ALMOST INFINITE UTILIZATION POSSIBILITIES

So how much underutilization is there really? Note that my humble paper clip might have slumbered in my desk drawer for 20 or 30 years, awaiting the one time when I might want to press it into service to hold a couple of pages together. I can't calculate the number of zeros in the utilization rate (0.000000001 percent). It is an outlier on the utilization front.

Or is it? The closer we look at many assets, the more we find that their utilization rates are infinitesimally small. *The more one slices and dices the property rights to an asset, the more utilization possibilities one discovers.*

Take my car, which admittedly is not used as often as many cars. One would expect that a car would be a relatively well-used asset compared to most of the assets that people possess. After four years of ownership and a crude estimate that we drive on average at 35 kilometers per hour (about 22 mph) in the city and suburbs, my estimate is that our car gets used on average for 25 minutes a day, which equates to a utilization rate of 1.7 percent.

When one slices and dices utilization, one finds wasteful underutilization everywhere. Most of the time there is only one person in the car's five seats. The trunk is empty during many rides. The engine is used below its potential, and there is no roof rack on it, which could be used as part of the last mile delivery economy. If it was an electric vehicle, when not in use, the battery could be rented out as an electricity storage device. With an increasing ability to slice and dice property rights and asset uses along all these dimensions, the utilization rate of one of my most valuable assets is probably well below 0.1 percent of its potential. Yet car sharing and ride-sharing are talked about as one of the early winners among the sharing economy. The game has barely begun; my car could be delivering many, many times more value or happiness to the world.

Of course, it will be hard to capture the full value from the grotesque underutilization of my car. But as TxCs fall, maybe my car will be part of the last mile comprehensive solution noted in the review of the tyranny of geography TxC that should be coming our way. Maybe when I specify a destination for my trip, a package will magically end up in my trunk and magically end up being taken out of my trunk when I get to my destination (or some intermediate point along the way). Maybe in an era of ubiquitous ride-sharing or a future world of self-driving cars, utilization of cars could go up 20- to 40-fold, to above 50 percent (and why not closer to 100 percent?). If so, the number of cars required will completely collapse. Assets will flow fluidly to their highest value usage.

While it is impossible to judge accurately the extent to which the weighted average value of our gross assets is underutilized, there is a good chance that they are used to less than 5 percent of their potential; it could be 1 percent, or even a fraction of 1 percent.

TECHNIQUE I:
ADOPTING DYNAMIC PRICING

The world of business seems to be divided into two major blocs. There are those sectors where prices are fixed, and those sectors where pricing is dynamic. We seem to have the sense that consumers will accept dynamic pricing for certain use cases and not for others.

We accept that companies flex prices in all most types of travel offerings—flights, hotels, car rental. Excess demand feeds into higher prices for a hotel room. Indeed, a hotel in a vacation spot might make all of its profit in the summer months and lose money the rest of the year, although it might justify staying open during the off season by making a small income that allows it to make a contribution to its fixed overhead.

A printing company might break even or lose money on most of the orders that it fulfills in a month. On those few occasions when someone shows up late on a Friday and needs an order filled immediately or needs something special done, it can price aggressively. This very high margin pricing on a tiny percentage of the orders might be what the printing company needs to make profit in a month.

Uber uses surge pricing to draw in drivers at time of high need and to decrease demand so that supply and demand can be brought back into balance. Without excellence in managing dynamic pricing, these travel companies and the printing company would simply not be able to make a profit. Turning that logic on its head, entrepreneurs can build valuable businesses if they can introduce dynamic pricing in a sector where the rest of the players are stuck in a fixed pricing model.

We see some basic attempts to flex pricing in the interests of boosting profitability:

* Restaurants split menus between lunch and dinner and extend the lunch period until 4 or 5 p.m. so that it doesn't catch any potential dinner-goers.
* Barbers offer cheap rates for seniors at dead times on Mondays and Tuesdays.

- Matinees in movie theaters are often extremely cheap to entice people through the door who might then buy drinks and popcorn.

With electronic shelf-edge labels, prices can now be changed very easily, taking away the hassles of updating the prices of many goods. It sounds like it is time for entrepreneurs to try out new propositions and test customers' willingness to pay flexible prices. This might include:

- Barbers flexing their prices in hourly blocks depending on projected demand
- Convenience supermarkets using time-of-day pricing
- Ice-cream shops moving to a surge pricing model at times of high demand
- B2B suppliers flexing pricing depending on stock-outs within suppliers
- Plumbers having a higher call-out charge at their prime times

Where else might it be possible to redesign a business proposition by switching out fixed prices in favor of dynamic prices?

CHAPTER 13

The Power of Swarms

One exciting aspect of the recent fall in TxCs is the emergence of many swarms. Swarms are groups of independent small-sized suppliers or buyers of goods or services where the whole is far more powerful than the sum of the parts. Working as a team enables them to lower TxCs on behalf of their customers in imaginative and valuable ways that they couldn't as independent suppliers. Think of Uber, Etsy, eBay, Upwork, merchants on Amazon, and associations of professionals.

For example, it is great if I have the phone number of a good, trustworthy driver who might be available to drive me to the airport or home from the pub. But it is even better if I can plug into a swarm of thousands of good, trustworthy drivers, and even better again if I can pinpoint the closest one and get her to pick me up in a few minutes or instantly. The lowering of TxCs via a functioning swarm turns a good, trustworthy driver into an on-demand service.

A SWARM—SELLERS OR BUYERS WORKING TOGETHER TO CRUSH TxCS

A swarm emerges when a group of sellers (or buyers) coordinates its members to provide a lower TxC service than they could by themselves. Seller (or buyer) coordination has a long history.

Take, for example, the concept of a franchise. A franchiser creates a new business model (e.g., a local laundry service) and builds the evidence case that this business model can yield a good profit to prospective franchisees. Building this evidence case might entail the franchiser setting up some laundry locations and bringing them to profitability. He or she then offers the same business model to others in return for some compensation (up-front money or a share in future revenues). The franchisee has the right to use the name of the franchise. The franchisee also agrees to a common set of operating rules that are aimed at maintaining the value of the franchise brand. These rules are important as they set minimum standards that must be met. It is then in the interests of all the members of the franchisee network to maintain standards and to ensure that their fellow franchisees maintain standards. All benefit as a result. Consumers can have more faith in the products or services delivered by the individual operators; trust is enhanced and exchange boosted.

You can see how important these types of operating rules are in, say, a chain of independently owned sandwich shops. The chain is stronger together—better branding, consistent products, quality and cleanliness standards, pricing alignment, wait times.

For centuries, people or firms bandied together into professional groups or associations into order to deliver a proposition to their desired counterparties that they wouldn't have been able to deliver by themselves. A professional association of accountants whose members have gone through formal training programs, exams, and continuing professional education can deliver up a swarm of members in whom counterparties can place high trust. Breach of this trust or of the standards of expected professional behavior can lead to fines or expulsion. It is in the interests of all the members to ensure that the bad eggs are reprimanded or ejected. With a swarm, the whole is better than the sum of the parts.

THE INTERNET SIMPLIFIES AND MULTIPLIES THE CREATION OF SWARMS

One of the early exciting benefits of the internet was the ability to search across the market; if you couldn't search across the market for buyers or sellers, your willingness to exchange was diminished. Assuming you could search, you still banged up against lots of other TxCs, such as lack of trust, geography, and payments friction if the suppliers or buyers were small and dispersed. Gathering all the suppliers together into a virtual swarm is now easy.

You might have been a collector of Pez dispensers well before the arrival of eBay; now, you live in a much happier world in which you can finally find someone in the swarm of eBay sellers with that rare Pez dispenser that you have been trying to locate for years. Your unfulfilled demand is encountering someone else's excess supply. eBay sorted out almost all the TxCs for you.

Some of the early swarms enabled by the internet included:

- **Amazon marketplace.** Third-party sellers make up roughly half of sales on Amazon, despite the high charges to the sellers. The reason the sellers are here is because this is where the buyers are.
- **eBay.** A swarm of buyers meets a swarm of sellers across the world.
- **Etsy.** It provides an outlet for the swarm of people in the maker community who separately would not have been able to gain the attention of individual buyers or a swarm of buyers.
- **Takeout ordering from restaurants.** You can now search across all the restaurants in your catchment area.
- **Takeout delivery.** The restaurants now have a swarm of drivers at their disposal.

Any sector in which there are lots of small sellers (or buyers) today and where buyers (or sellers) face significant TxCs in the exchange offers a good opportunity for the creation of a swarm. These sectors might include personal services (hair, etc.), home repair, and the various aspects of the sharing economy.

HOW SWARMS CAN LOWER TxCS

Once a swarm is in place, there are many ways in which they can reduce TxCs for their counterparties that they couldn't do if they were to continue operating independently.

Swarms Facilitate Easier Search

Why would I, as a provider of a good or service, want my customers to be able to search across the market and, in the process, find one of my competitors from the swarm to work with? Well, I don't really want it (especially if I am a dominant current player), but counterparties often want this ability to search and exchange may be inhibited unless they get it. If a swarm forms that allows the counterparties to search across the market, then I had better be a part of it. If Amazon Marketplace is where products like mine are being sold, then I had better be on Amazon, despite all the competition.

Most swarms allow me to search far and wide using whatever criteria I want to use. Flight aggregators like Kayak or Skyscanner allow me to search along previously unheard of dimensions such as stopover time, flight leg length, connecting cities, and airlines. My ability to search is almost limitless, and most of the market for flights is at my fingertips. My ability to conduct such a broad and occasionally idiosyncratic search means that I have a better chance at meeting my needs. The airlines might not like being compared so pointedly price-to-price as this inhibits their ability to win using their brand or other nonprice factors, but the alternative of not being on flight aggregator or comparison websites and missing possible customers is not appealing. Similarly, If I wanted takeout food a few years ago, I had to call up my favorite local restaurant and swing by to pick it up (assuming they didn't deliver—and other than pizza joints, few did). Now I can open an app called Just Eat (in the UK) or DoorDash or Uber Eats or Grubhub and search across a swarm of restaurants—probably finding a bunch I had never heard of before. One feature of swarms is that there are increasing returns to scale. More restaurants on the platform means more consumers, which means that the remaining undecided restaurants get sucked in onto the platform over time. For the consumer, it is a great experience—a searchable database that allows us to discover the Indonesian restaurant that we had never heard about. Then to get the food delivered, I can access a swarm of delivery drivers who are managed algorithmically to deliver my food as fast as possible.

Swarms Inject Trust into the Exchange

Swarms impose common standards on members, on pain of expulsion if they don't live up to those expected standards. All participants protect their ratings (normally 4 out of 5 is the minimum expectation), and a collection of good reviews engenders trust. We reviewed earlier how the existence of the swarm made it possible for people and drivers to build up a level of trust in each other sufficient to allow them to ride-share in a manner almost unthinkable only 10 or so years ago.

Swarms Make the Exchange Possible

Swarms allow counterparties to contract with members of the swarm seamlessly. I don't need to negotiate with the ride-sharing driver. I can have a relationship with the swarm curator to strike the bargain with the provider. Returning to the food delivery example, we get a set of value-added services bundled in, such as predicted delivery times, driving tracking via GPS, preregistered address information, and specific directions.

Swarms Facilitate the Transfer of Value

After the product is delivered or the service performed, the payment can be initiated through the coordinator swarm easily without the counterparties having to fuss over the details.

"CURATED" SWARMS VERSUS VIRTUAL SWARMS

Beware those who want to control the swarm. The most prominent swarms that we have seen so far in the internet era typically have one commercially minded, self-interested party in the middle that designs the platform, sets the standards, handles recruitment of the members, builds trust by facilitating reviews and ratings, strikes the implicit or explicit contract between the swarm member and the counterparty, and ensures payment. They are the TxC crushers.

For these services, the curator (Uber, Airbnb, Amazon Merchant Services, Just Eat, etc.) often takes 20 percent of the value of the transaction. Swarm participants have had to accept that this "tax" on exchange (a true monetary TxC) is worth it. Being outside the swarm is a cold place. Over time, perhaps the swarm members will take back the power and seek to bypass the curator (and the 20 percent fee) and move to some sort of virtual open-source platform that continues to deliver the best of what the swarms have done to reduce TxCs.

SWARMS WILL WIN IN MOST INSTANCES

Swarms benefit from network scale economics whereby $N + 1$ members make the service better than if there are N members. The more drivers there are on Uber, the better the service for users due to the lower wait time. Drivers also are making countless small self-optimizing decisions regarding which hours to work, where to hang out, when to take breaks. Drivers become micro-entrepreneurs working tirelessly to improve their own enterprise—improving their ratings by keeping their car clean, being on time, being courteous. It will be nearly impossible for a hierarchal player (such as a national postal service) to compete once the swarm gets going.

Some buyers might shrug off the value of a swarm, saying, "I have my favorite barber, and I'll be sticking with him." That may well be the case, but the swarm can still be useful—I can see what new barbers are in the area; I can see their prices; if there is online ordering I can guarantee my slot and avoid wasted time; I can pay very simply. The swarm's advantages erode the historic relationship benefits with small providers, and the swarm tend to suck in holdouts over time.

TECHNIQUE J:
CONSTRUCTING A SWARM

The owners of proprietary swarms are in a very powerful position:

* There are increasing returns to scale with each additional participant that joins.
* Swarms are incredibly hard to dislodge once they are in place.
* They offer a great proposition to their customers.

The good news is that there are many opportunities to create swarms. The obvious first targets such as ride-sharing, short-term accommodation, food delivery, etc. have been done, but there are many to go. Theoretically, every small business might be part of a swarm.

Retail Offerings

A good way to start unearthing possible future swarms is to walk around and see which small independent proprietors still exist. The shopping area closest to my home has the following (non-chain) merchants:

* Jewelry and accessories
* Coffee shop
* Optometrist
* Greeting cards
* Secondhand electronics trading
* Hearing testing
* Bra and swimwear sizing
* Dry cleaner
* Gallery
* Kids' clothes
* Butcher
* Barber
* Vaping
* Electronic repair
* Dentist

- Schoolbooks
- Chiropractor
- Library
- Gym

Does it make sense to pick one of these areas and start creating a swarm around it? The goal is not simply to get small businesses to create a club; the goal is to completely recreate the customer experience by wiping out all the TxCs associated with the service today in a way that one provider couldn't by himself or herself.

Could we create a swarm of chiropractors? As someone who has never used a chiropractor, I have a long list of TxCs in the form of questions that prevent me from even considering using the service:

- How do I know when I should seek help from a chiropractor?
- How much does it cost, and how often does one need to go?
- How do I know if the chiropractor I am considering using is any good or not?
- Is there a standard set of chiropractor procedures for dealing with each type of issue that a person might present with? What does a successful treatment entail?
- What hours are they open, and does that work for my busy schedule? Will they come to my home?
- When should I use a physiotherapist and when a chiropractor?

Does it make sense for a group of chiropractors to come together to form a swarm and overcome all my objections? Would this open an enormous latent market for underutilized chiropractor services?

Household and Personal Services

Could certain household and personal services be ripe for conversion to a swarm? Plumbers, electricians, equipment servicing, gutter cleaning, house painting, tree cutters, gardeners, chimney cleaning: the list of householder services could be 10 times longer. What about personal services such as haircutting, physiotherapy, pedicure, dentistry, and dental cleaning? These are all services where consumers face many TxCs—trust issues, price uncertainty, payments issues, ability to pinpoint and contract with providers, etc. Often the most important TxC is the opportunity cost of the customers' time. My time is pretty valuable to me, and I would prefer these household and personal services to work around my schedule rather than the reverse.

Swarms in the World of Business

Many businesses use groups of people as part of their own delivery system. Are there ways to turn these groups into TxC reduction swarms that enhance the company's proposition?

Take the repairs and after-service departments of many firms. Many businesses have an in-house team of repair people ready to address customers' problems. Perhaps this team could become the kernel of a swarm that becomes independent and entrepreneurial and works to lower TxCs for customers.

Similarly for sales departments. Many businesses have teams of in-house salespeople or a cadre of captive agents or a set of independent brokers or resellers. Maybe these teams could take on the characteristics and benefits of a swarm. Other swarms might be possible for groups of installers, customer support people, and delivery people.

One advantage for businesses in turning in-house teams into affiliated swarms is that the activity moves from strictly being a cost center to one where the swarm comprises loosely affiliated participants who act almost like independent entrepreneurs. Could the swarm evolve from one that just serves one business (on a subscale basis) to one that serves multiple businesses? This would put the original business owner into the powerful position of being the curator of the swarm.

CHAPTER 14

Should Firms Do Tasks Inside the Hierarchy or Pass Them Outside to Entrepreneurs?

W hat tasks should a firm do itself, and which tasks should it let a third party do? This is an important question for the design of a firm.

Ronald Coase, who is widely considered to be the father of the Theory of the Firm, observed that firms will expand or shrink until the cost of making something equals the cost of buying it.* In effect, would it cost less to do things in-house rather than getting someone else to do it?

The CEO of the firm, whether a startup firm or a Fortune 500 company, is the de facto architect of the firm's organization. The first (but not the only) structural decision facing the architect of the firm is deciding which tasks should be done by the firm, and which ones should be sourced from third parties. In other words, where exactly should the boundary of the firm be?

The answer to this question is, you guessed, that it depends largely on the TxCs. The relevant TxCs in this case would include the costs of identifying potential trading partners, negotiating contracts, monitoring for compliance, and so on. You will see how TxCs for firms mirror those suffered by individuals. For

---

* Ronald Coase, "The Nature of the Firm," *Journal of Law, Organisation and Economics*, 1937.

simplicity, let's define TxCs as the hassles of dealing with other firms. If firm A finds that there are lots of hassles associated with having firms B, C, and D undertake tasks for it, then firm A will, on balance, undertake those tasks through its own hierarchy. If there are few hassles, firm A will outsource many tasks.

TxCs act as inhibitors to trade with other firms, thereby coaxing or forcing the firm to keep a process, an employee, or a skill in-house. If we don't have trust in counterparties, we are less likely to trade with them.

ONE EXTREME: TINY TxCS PROVIDE ENORMOUS OPPORTUNITIES FOR ENTREPRENEURS

In a zero-TxC world, everything can be bought simply and fluidly through the price mechanism in a market. Other firms (let's call them entrepreneurs), offer their goods and services, and buyers can know that they are getting exactly what they want. The buyer also has relatively perfect information on these entrepreneurs—a "broadband" view into their operations (e.g., expected delivery times, impending supply bottlenecks, quality stats).

If every task can be sourced seamlessly (with tiny TxCs) through the market mechanism from entrepreneurs, then theoretically each firm only needs to comprise one individual or one task or process. Indeed, not only can virtually all tasks be done by third-party entrepreneurs (disaggregated to the lowest level)—everything *should* be done by third parties. Tasks should be fulfilled by firms or people in line with the principles of comparative advantage. Chapter 15 will discuss specialization and why this is the case.

To an economist's eye, the market represents an "ocean of unconscious co-operation."* Participants can exchange in a no-TxC manner. None of the participants in such a disaggregated supply chain needs to own the whole chain. They can work in

---

* D. H. Robertson, quoted in Ronald Coase, "The Nature of the Firm."

unison without much conscious thought required. If I buy 250 green hoodies here in Dublin, computers across the world might stir themselves to note that nugget of information and start considering how the unexpected purchase of that many green hoodies will impact the supply chain for cotton, drawstrings, green dye, or buttons in multiple countries across the globe. The unconscious cooperation across global supply chains for something like the humble hoodie is simply amazing.

A fully disaggregated world in which everyone exchanges fluidly through the market is nirvana for entrepreneurs—there are essentially infinite new opportunities to exchange with other parties fluidly. All the entrepreneur needs to do is to become best-in-class at a specific task!

THE OTHER EXTREME: ENORMOUS TxCS PROVIDE FEW OPPORTUNITIES FOR ENTREPRENEURS

Imagine a world where there is zero trust in anyone other than "us," where information on your potential counterparties is extremely difficult to get, and where there is no ability to coordinate and monitor the work or activities of other firms and entrepreneurs, such that we can't ensure that their work isn't shoddy. In such a high-TxC world, firms will tend to do most tasks in-house, through their hierarchy.

Acting through the hierarchy of the firm (as opposed to buying through the market) implies that there are managers who coordinate the tasks—in effect, someone in charge who must make trade-off decisions. They are "islands of conscious power in this ocean of unconscious co-operation."*

The alternative for the firm might be to put in place a complex contract with a third party. A contract might not be possible to draft if the situation is dynamic and it is challenging or impossible to develop a contract sufficiently robust to handle the situation.

---

* D. H. Robertson, quoted in Ronald Coase, "The Nature of the Firm."

Firms may thus be seen as a vessel for holding together the people and tasks required to deliver a product or service offering in a high-TxC situation when relying on others doesn't make sense. The firm becomes a "nexus of contracts"*—each person connected to the firm (employees, managers, senior executives, etc.) has a bilateral contract with the firm and is, effectively, inside the hierarchy. This allows the firm to direct the person to do what the firm wants him or her to do.

Unfortunately, a world of enormous TxCs means there is virtually no opportunity for entrepreneurship. Enormous TxCs lead to enormous hierarchies, and everything is done within the firm.

○ ○ ○

This is the essence of the Theory of the Firm: What tasks are in versus what are out, and consequently, what is the boundary of the firm? The key choice for the firm architect is whether a task is undertaken within the firm (through the hierarchy) or whether it is undertaken through the market. The worlds of extremes— zero TxCs and enormous TxCs—help to illuminate this choice.

The existence of a hierarchy with more than one task implies that there is some problem with using the market mechanism. It might be lack of trust in the other party. It might also be a lack of a good contract that addresses the various circumstances that arise between the two parties; it might that the hierarchy is worried that it would become too dependent on the other party over time. In short, there are TxCs. Whatever the reason, the firm believes it is better off keeping that task within the hierarchy and avoiding having to exchange with a third party, even though that third party might be better (faster, cheaper, etc.) at the task than the firm itself.

In Chapter 15, we will look at why disaggregation is an irresistible force driving value—taking tasks out of a firm and handing them to an entrepreneur who can do them better.

---

* Martin Ricketts, *The Economics of Business Enterprise*, 3rd ed. (United Kingdom: Edward Elgar Publishing, 2002), 43.

Specialization Blows Hierarchies Apart, Showering the World with Entrepreneurial Opportunities

The enormous productivity improvement offered by specialization, also known as the division of labor, is the economic driving force behind the relentless disaggregation of tasks. Without specialization, there is no impetus to "give birth" to a new firm outside of our current hierarchy. This possibility of disaggregation is what gets our budding entrepreneurs out of bed.

WHAT IS SPECIALIZATION (DIVISION OF LABOR)?

Division of labor is "the assignment of different parts of a process or task to different people in order to improve efficiency."* Specialization means that different people or groups undertake different tasks rather than one person or group carrying out the whole process. Here is a simple example: Assume that we have 10 people making shoes. We have at least two choices for how to organize those 10 people. We could have each person make

---

* https://languages.oup.com/google-dictionary-en/.

a whole shoe by themselves, or we could have each of the 10 specialize. With specialization one person might cut the leather uppers, another might cut the soles, another might punch the holes for the laces, another might sew the pieces together, and another might lace up the shoes.

Adam Smith gave the simple example of pin making. At the time he wrote *The Wealth of Nations*, he observed that the making of a pin could be broken into 16 distinct steps to be undertaken by 10 different people. These 10 men could make 48,000 pins per day. One worker, if he or she were to make pins alone, would be lucky to make one pin in a day.

Over time, specialization has proven to yield enormous productivity improvements. Ten people might individually make a small number of shoes or pins each in a day, but the 10 operating in a specialized manner could make hundreds or thousands of shoes or pins.

Unsurprisingly, we experience the world of work as one of increasing specialization. We have specialized jobs for people whose job titles today didn't exist only a few years ago. Perusing the job boards for people with software skills, we can find jobs for backend developers, Android developers, IOS developers, full-stack developers, lead developers, user interface specialists, data scientists, machine learning specialists, and typescript developers—none of which were around before the continued application of specialization to software development. *Capturing the value offered by specialization is the main driving force in the design of organizations.*

DIVISION OF LABOR CAN LEAD TO UNIMAGINABLE INCREASES IN PRODUCTIVITY

While people can understand, intuitively, the advantage of dividing labor, they tend to miss that the division of labor leads to quite staggering increases in productivity. Specialization does not just lead to a doubling of productivity; it can lead to a many thousandfold increase in productivity.

The reasons why specialization leads to remarkable productivity increases are fairly straightforward to understand. The task becomes simplified and can be done repetitively. The setup effort each time the task is to be undertaken is eliminated. The task benefits from economics of scale. Workers can become more adept at the task over time. Specialized workers can be smart about inventing new ways of making the task easier and faster to undertake. The task becomes more susceptible to being automated through software.

This is why dividing labor leads to enormous productivity improvements. There is a reason I don't grow all my own vegetables—I can go to the grocery store and get a bag of carrots for less than a Euro from a farmer who has grown untold tons of them.

SOFTWARE IS INFINITELY SCALABLE

Software has the unique property that it is "write once, use often." Once written, it (theoretically) has no marginal cost. It can scale infinitely. An infinitely scalable worker is a powerful one.

The economics of taking a task currently performed by a human and turning it over to a software program are very compelling. As a result, every task in a firm should be under intense scrutiny from people and entrepreneurs who want to automate it with software. Think of any corporate process or task and run it through a search engine. The chances are that there are firms out there that have created a software program or app to automate it.

Look at typical tasks in the domain of managing employees. Every big company used to have an army of people, operating in a relatively nonspecialized manner to do the following tasks (among many others):

* Manage the process of employee recruitment
* Onboard new staff administratively
* Process and check employee expenses
* Enroll staff in pension plans and medical plans

A small firm might have one or two of its staff collectively doing all these tasks, inefficiently. A bigger firm might have a large team of staff broken out across these areas. The bigger the firm, the more opportunity to reduce the unit cost of each task completed. Over time this bigger firm might automate some of the tasks via software to improve the unit cost of completing the task even more.

THE POTENTIAL GAINS TO SPECIALIZATION ARE LIMITED BY THE SIZE OF THE MARKET FOR THE PROCESS

Eventually, the impetus for specialization within a hierarchical firm runs out. Why bother writing a software program to enroll staff in medical plans if the additional cost of writing the program is bigger than the efficiencies to be captured by a lower unit cost per task undertaken? This is the conundrum that ultimately leads to the disaggregation of the firm.

There is a task within a firm that is ripe for specialization; let's use the example of enrolling people in medical plans. On a unit cost basis, it could be made more efficient if it were subject to the division of labor, either getting a specialist person in to run it, or writing some software to automate the process. But that doesn't happen: the "market" within the hierarchical firm is not big enough to justify the division of labor, and there are not enough staff to be enrolled in medical plans to justify committing a team to the task of writing software to automate the task.

The size of the potential market determines the extent to which the division of labor and specialization can be pursued and limits the productivity gains. When the only possible customers are in the hierarchy itself, the opportunities derived from the division of labor is limited by the size of the firm.

THUS THE IMPERATIVE FOR SPECIALIZATION AND DISAGGREGATION

All tasks have an inbuilt engine that drives them toward specialization. Humans, especially entrepreneurs, want to make tasks more efficient (to decrease costs and thus make more money), and the fundamental way this happens is through specialization. When we reach the limits of specialization within the "internal market size" of a particular firm, there is only one way for the specialization to keep going—we need to increase the size of the target market. We need to take the task out of the firm and give it the chance to play in a bigger value pool. It needs to serve many or even all firms. This could be through a spinout of a process from the firm into a new entrepreneurial entity (perhaps owned by the original firm). The more likely scenario is that an external entrepreneur sees the opportunity to create a lower cost per unit, more on-demand offering than the hierarchy can deliver to itself, and then develops it.

The economic tension between specialization of tasks and TxCs sets the boundary of the firm.

o o o

In summary, we have the powerful, relentless economic force of specialization that aims to multiply value by disaggregating tasks running headlong into the joy-killers of economic prosperity—our old friends, TxCs, which exist to inhibit disaggregation and trade between firms.

We know already who has the upper hand in this epic tussle. Specialization is finally getting the chance to run rampant as TxCs are falling fast. The glue that has held tasks together within the boundaries of the firm is coming undone. The construct of the firm is becoming much more fluid—almost every task within a firm is suddenly up for salami-slicing into a separate entrepreneurial opportunity. Opportunities for entrepreneurs in disaggregation are multiplying.

GETTING MICRO: SHOULD A FIRM DISAGGREGATE A SPECIFIC TASK OR NOT?

The momentum toward specialization is a chain reaction. The more specialization happens, the more possibilities for specialization emerge. Specialized tasks get divided into specialized subtasks, which then enable further specialization at the next task level. Each specialization reaction in turn releases powerful amounts of productivity and value.

As we specialize within the firm, we can quickly reach the limits of demand—the quantity that the hierarchy requires for its own purposes. Maybe a clothing firm only needs 1,000 pins per day to satisfy its own demand. If so, in theory it could decide to specialize anyway and sell the excess 47,000 pins per day on the market. The next question that arises is, why is the firm even making pins? It isn't in the pin business; it's a clothing company. Is there a firm out there with a specialized process that is making 48 billion pins a day with, say, 20 workers? Their cost per pin should be much less than ours. Let's disaggregate that task and just exchange with them. Instead of every company making its own pins, let's create or promote or support a pin-making entrepreneurial opportunity for someone else.

While the productivity benefits of disaggregating pin making might be attractive, we start bumping up against the TxCs that make disaggregation less appealing. Maybe pins are important to our business and relying on the market to deliver a supply of pins exactly when we want them, at a consistently reliable price, makes us a bit nervous. How do we make the decision to disaggregate a specific task or not?

A Simple Example: A Pizza Making and Delivery Company

ABC Pizza makes pizzas and delivers them to people's homes—a two-task process. In reality, the making of the pizza could be disaggregated into subtasks for different people—making the dough, preparing the toppings, putting on the toppings, loading pizzas into the oven, and packing the pizza in a box. Similarly, the delivery of the pizza could be disaggregated into subtasks such as picking up pizzas, driving them, delivering them, and, maybe, accepting payment. For our purposes, let's assume it is a simple two-task process.

The owner of ABC Pizza has a decision: Does she keep it as a single firm, aggregated across both the making and delivering of pizzas, or does she disaggregate the delivery of the pizzas to a third party?

If the theory of specialization is correct, then absent TxCs, it should make sense to specialize in the making of pizzas and specialize separately in the delivering of pizzas. If we disaggregate the delivery of pizzas, we dramatically increase the size of the potential market for delivery. Before, the "market" for delivery within the aggregated ABC Pizza firm was pretty small—it was just the pizzas made by ABC. After disaggregation, we have the potential to deliver pizzas or food for other restaurants. We have higher volume, so the economics of specialization can get us a lower cost, better delivery operation. The delivery firm will probably have a denser series of deliveries (e.g., multiple deliveries per trip), and it may have more sophisticated routing capabilities that allow it to lower its cost per delivery. It is not hard to believe that a delivery firm that is making a huge number of deliveries (a multiple of the delivery count of any one restaurant) should be able to achieve a very low cost per delivery. Because it has more drivers, it should be able to offer a more on-demand service, with drivers being quicker to pick up pizzas and deliver them hotter.

In summary, the forces of specialization would suggest that disaggregation makes sense. Now, however, we run into the TxCs of disaggregation.

The owner of the pizzeria is likely to have TxC concerns running through her head along the following lines: Will the delivery firm be reliable? Will they care about our customers? What happens if there is a service delivery problem (e.g., someone drops a pizza)? Will the delivery company start by offering us low rates (per delivery or per hour) and then raise them later when we become more dependent on them? On the other hand, not employing delivery drivers means fewer headaches to manage. What happens if there is a particularly busy night—the delivery firm will probably be better at scaling up capacity than if the pizza maker managed the delivery workforce itself.

The task of the delivery entrepreneur is clear: specialize more and offer a great service. Minimize the pickup times; use smart routing software and deliver the pizzas faster and hotter than

ABC Pizza could deliver them. Become skilled at handling service problems such as dropped pizzas. Be able to redeploy staff from other customers at short notice, for example, if demand for pizzas is high because of a big game on TV. Provide great online dashboards showing where all the drivers are. Crush every TxC in sight.

We now have two entrepreneurs rather than one, with more potential for productivity and value.

CHAPTER 16

The Complete Disaggregation of the Firm over Time

I n Chapter 15, we covered the value of disaggregation of a task from a firm as well as an example of how one company (a pizza firm) might decide to disaggregate one task. Here, we will explore how, over the long term, firms are going to become completely disaggregated and how this will create opportunities for entrepreneurs.

Figure 16.1 characterizes a firm with the tasks it undertakes. These tasks are within the boundary of the firm.

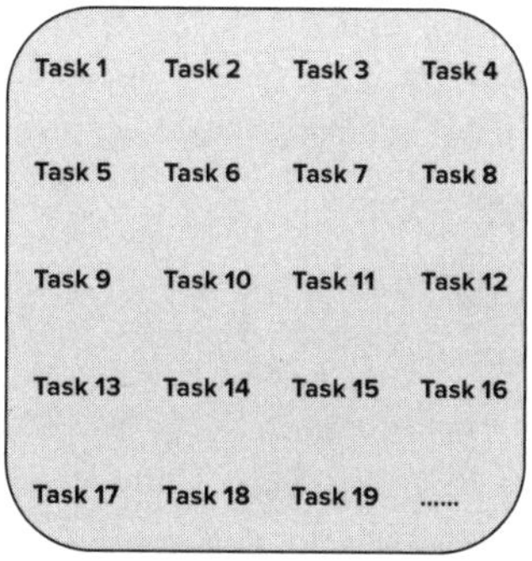

Task 1	Task 2	Task 3	Task 4
Task 5	Task 6	Task 7	Task 8
Task 9	Task 10	Task 11	Task 12
Task 13	Task 14	Task 15	Task 16
Task 17	Task 18	Task 19	......

Figure 16.1 The Tasks Undertaken by a Company

THE DISAGGREGATION JOURNEY SO FAR

In the nineteenth century, the bulk of a firm's tasks were conducted inside the firm. Firms were highly vertically integrated. They had to be, as few reliable suppliers were available. In fact, many firms even built housing for their workers, covering the TxCs associated with the lack of public transportation. Workers had to live near the factories to be able to get to work, resulting in the narrow streets of brick row housing in the cities that were early hosts to the industrial revolution. In the early spirit of disaggregation, as the TxCs of worker transportation came down, factory owners could happily outsource the provision of worker housing and let workers mediate through the market for their own housing.

So began the journey of moving tasks out of the firm (Figure 16.2) to capture the productivity benefits of specialization that were not capturable by the hierarchy of the firm due to the limitations of a firm's demand for the task. The first tasks moved out were ones that could easily be purchased through the market—where TxCs were low.

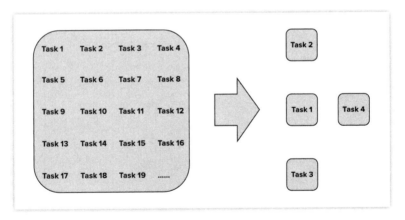

Figure 16.2 The Start of the Process of
Moving Tasks Out of the Firm

Some of the early tasks to be moved outside of the firm are obvious to us with the wisdom of hindsight. Why on earth would a firm:

- Generate its own electricity?
- Provide meals to staff?
- Be its own cleaning service?
- Provide transportation to and from work?
- Be its own telecom provider?

These are no-brainers to us; there are wonderful, reliable on-demand services available to most firms that don't require a complicated contract to ensure the firm gets its needs fulfilled. Then we start getting into processes and tasks that are on the way to becoming on-demand services that the firm will be able to get through the market, to the extent that they can't already. These include reception service (digital or in person), secretarial services, executive coaching, call centers, online- or phone-based lead generation for the sales force, product design, recruitment, branding and advertising, payroll, employee benefits management, software development for internal processes, inbound and outbound transportation, etc. The list could be endless. More and more happy days for entrepreneurs looking to build a specialized business focused on one of these tasks.

While your initial reaction might be, "Well, those are only support services that are not that central to the real business of a firm," this belies the fact that most tasks that companies undertake are relatively mundane, and when looked at individually it is hard to argue that they are mission-critical to the firm. Most are just tasks that need to get done, and the more efficiently they are done, the better. The orchestration of the tasks is what matters, rather than the tasks themselves.

Outsourcing some or all the production tasks within a company tends to raise concerns. If a firm outsources all of its production capabilities, there is a good argument that doing so may inhibit its ability to innovate at a product level. If this is the case, it implies a major TxC associated with outsourcing that needs to be considered.

Apple is an example of a highly disaggregated firm. In 2020 it earned gross margins of 38 percent on its total sales, after which it spent 7 percent of sales on research and development (R&D) and 7 percent on administration, yielding a very appealing net margin on sales of 24 percent. It is an R&D company that designs smartphones, tablets, and other electronics, markets them, and then passes virtually all other tasks, including production, to the market.

THE LONG JOURNEY TOWARD TOTAL DISAGGREGATION

Let's start by looking at things from the perspective of the infinite horizon. In a world of zero TxCs, firms move toward total disaggregation as more specialization drives tasks to ever higher levels of productivity.

Zero TxCs means that it is as easy to trade with another firm as it is to undertake a task within the firm. Therefore, one would always aim to exchange with the best-in-class supplier of that task, a supplier that is fully specialized and achieves the best possible economies of scale.

With total disaggregation, the firm as we know it is no longer. Each task is separated and coordinates with all the other activities seamlessly—in fact, no coordination effort should be required. A different firm might own each task. Total disaggregation reimagines the firm as something like Figure 16.3.

On first blush, one might think that the amount of coordination required between the completely disaggregated parties on the right side of the image would be overwhelming. That underestimates the ability of current software technologies—open-source software platforms, easily accessible application programming interfaces (APIs), etc., never mind future technologies—to coordinate activities through the unconscious cooperation of the market.

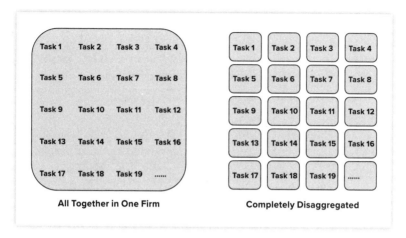

Figure 16.3 Disaggregation Taken to Its Extreme

In fact, hints of the disaggregated firm of the future are already with us, albeit in simplistic form for fairly homogenous tasks. Take the traditional delivery business. The immense complexity of such a business has over the years been managed through the hierarchy, and enormous levels of coordination are required. Firms like the US Postal Service and the Royal Mail in the United Kingdom perform herculean coordination of their incredibly complex operations.

In glimpsing the future through the eyes of early players such as Uber and Deliveroo (UK), things look likely to be very different. It is possible that we will have a disaggregated business system with each node in the system considering itself an entrepreneur of sorts. All the coordination happens through a software platform, effectively eliminating all the coordination costs and internal TxCs of the traditional businesses. It is not just that the costs of coordination incurred by traditional hierarchical firms far outweighs any coordination costs of the new decentralized players. It is also, in the case of Uber, that the drivers are individual entrepreneurs aiming to optimize their performance by being in the right place at the right time to get better rides and by increasing their trust rating as much as possible. They also value the policing of their colleagues by the swarm—untrustworthy drivers hurt everyone. At some level they are like franchisees; they might not like all the rules, but they like the idea that service delivery demands are placed on all the driver franchisees to maintain common standards for customers.

It is not hard to believe that, as TxCs fall, the business model of the disaggregated players will supersede the traditional one. The nodes on the disaggregated players are entrepreneurial; more importantly, they are specialized. Additionally, as we discussed in earlier chapters, they are often working from positions of marginal cost economics and idle inventory. There are simply too many coordination costs demanding to be paid by the aggregated firm. Unless government intervenes to protect the traditional providers or, as is more likely, to slow down their demise, the future is not bright for these providers. In theory, they could try to transform themselves into disaggregated organisms, but the change management challenges to achieve this are overwhelming.

WHAT ABOUT CORPORATE STRATEGY AND CORE COMPETENCES?

The current predominant view in corporate strategy suggests that a firm must define, cultivate, and exploit its core competences to beat the competition. These core competences are the resources and capabilities that give the firm a strategic advantage and allow it to earn outsize returns.

Strategy: Focus on Core Competences

In "The Core Competence of the Corporation," the authors, C. K. Prahalad and Gary Hamel, posit that a company should focus on those competences that it can do uniquely well and that its competitors will have difficulty copying.* The company should nurture these core competences and outsource (or give less focus to) the other tasks in the business.

They laid down three tests for core competences:

1. **Relevance.** The competence must deliver something to a firm's customers that they really value.
2. **Difficulty in imitation.** This means that a firm can maintain its competitive advantage.
3. **Breadth of application.** The best type of competences are extensible to new areas.

Such core competences provide growth opportunities over time. Firms should be continually switching effort away from areas of weakness and toward areas of strength.

Is Prahalad and Hamel's view of corporate strategy incompatible with the view that we are on a relentless arc toward disaggregation of all tasks? At a superficial level, the two schools of thought are fairly consistent—firms should focus on what they are good at. A more contentious issue might be: Does the corporation really need to own the core competence? Could it not disaggregate it and access it from another firm?

Let's return to the simplified view of Apple as an R&D firm with a great brand and good marketing that has disaggregated all other activities to other providers. Its core competence is the design of smartphones and other devices. If, tomorrow, Apple finds a design company in Cairo that it believes is the best placed to develop the phones of the future—even better than Apple itself—should it think about disaggregating that R&D

---

* C. K. Prahalad and G. Hamel, "The Core Competence of the Corporation," *Harvard Business Review*, May-June1990, https://hbr.org/1990/05/the-core-competence-of-the-corporation.

capability? No doubt, there are severe TxCs associated with such a decision: Will the Cairo company steal the ideas and sell them to others? Does the balance of power shift in favor of the Cairo team over time? How does Apple "control" the design company's work without killing its creative genius? These are all issues that, in theory, can be gnawed away as TxCs fall.

A company like Apple is a long way away from thinking about disaggregating its product development, which is probably its true core competence. On the other hand, if we disaggregate product development itself into (1) product imagining (the truly creative aspect), and (2) software and hardware product development (the nuts and bolts of the engineering and technology development), maybe the idea of disaggregating task 2 is less unthinkable.

Firms don't necessarily need to own and undertake their own core competences. In the same way that Uber and Airbnb are ringmasters for their swarms of like-minded drivers, so companies can be ringmasters pulling together competences from different providers.

That said, disaggregation tends to start at the periphery of the firm and eat its way to the core. There are many worthwhile candidates for disaggregation to explore long before firms need to start considering core competences, such as Apple's design capability.

CHAPTER 17

Txcs and Disaggregation in the World of Banking

I
n the world of consumers, we identified eight primary categories of TxCs. In the world of business, the TxCs are extremely
situation- and sector-specific and not as easily categorized. In
this chapter we will examine TxCs in the banking sector.

The concept of an aggregated (vertically integrated) bank
has been a normal part of our lives for the past 100 years or
so. We think nothing of getting savings, payments, mortgages,
credit cards, or foreign exchange from the same place as companies raise loans, finance their assets, and hold their deposits.
Bundling and coordination between the different products
and end-to-end customer relationship management have been
among the key differentiating factors that banks have utilized
to capture and hold customers. However, using aggregation as a
customer proposition appears like it may be a losing hand for the
bank of the future. The powerful TxCs that have been holding
the aggregated bank together are falling away.

The economic forces driving disaggregation constitute the
biggest threat that banking (in the form in which we tradition-
ally conceive it) has ever faced. The disaggregation that it is
facing is not internally driven, "elective" disaggregation by the
bank hoping to capture the value of specializing certain tasks. It
is disaggregation led by hyperaggressive third parties (so-called
fintechs) that want to "salami-slice" and take over the most

profitable parts of the aggregated banks, leaving the banks with a husk of costly branches, outdated core banking systems, and an inflexible hierarchy.

Txcs IN THE WORLD OF BANKING

While, like all companies, there are a range of TxCs tentatively holding tasks together, there are two primary ones in banking—trust and government regulation.

Trust

Banking is based on one all-pervasive transaction benefit—trust. People and companies aim to earn a decent yield on their financial assets (knowing that they can suffer losses if they make unwise investments). They do not want to lose their assets as a result of the instability or poor management of the entity to which they have entrusted their precious assets. In most countries, people and companies do not need to worry about the safety of their financial assets in banks—the institutions have been solid repositories of assets for many decades.

Furthermore, governments regulate these entities and provide a guarantee to their customers. It can be an explicit guarantee in the form of account protections up to a limit of, say, $250,000 per depositor per government-insured bank (as in the United States), or an implicit guarantee if the financial institution mismanages itself or suffers a severe external shock—in either case with the government or central bank stepping in to bail out depositors.

These measures promulgate trust in banks, which is critical for entities with mismatched timing of their assets and liabilities that would not be able to pay off their depositors if they all showed up today looking for their money. Trust is the biggest TxC that entrepreneurs in the financial services sector need to overcome.

As we discussed earlier, trust is spreading in the world, and smart entrepreneurs can now craft new ways for customers and suppliers to build trust. For example, a fintech might decide to offer a new form of transaction or product to a customer (e.g., a really simplified way to execute foreign exchange transactions) and, having built up a decent customer base using this simple transaction (and engendered some trust), can extend the small bit of trust that has been earned into new product areas. We will cover the opportunities for reaggregation in Chapter 19.

Government Regulation

Governments provide protection for depositors (and provide a liquidity backstop); to avoid that protection being activated, they suppress competition for the banks. One way they suppress competition is by making entry into the sector heavily restricted. This slows the pace of change in the sector and mitigates the risk of the government having to pay out under their implicit underwriting of the sector. They also get to regulate the financial institutions.

Governments and regulatory authorities are slowly becoming more open to the process of adapting the regulatory systems to facilitate new entrants. Licenses to operate are being granted to new players, and experimentation with new business models is starting to happen. This is a slow process—as it probably should be, given the danger of failures among the new business models—people's money needs to be protected. There is a recognition that fossilizing the financial services sector and preventing innovation is not the best long-term approach.

○ ○ ○

As a result of these two powerful TxCs, the waves of change that have been washing through other sectors such as retail, travel, hospitality, and digital services have only started to lap at the door of aggregated banks.

DIFFERENT STRATEGIES OF FINTECHS

In this section, we will examine how the direct monetary TxCs and the intermediation margin that together represent the primary revenues of banks will be under pressure. Also, we will look at how the various tasks undertaken by a bank to deliver an aggregated product offering will also be peeled away into specialized, high-productivity stand-alone businesses.

Lining up against the traditional financial institutions are a vast array of entrepreneurial ventures, commonly known as *fintechs*. Fintechs can be arranged into three broad categories:

- Fintechs going directly after monetary TxCs earned by banks
- Fintechs working to compete away intermediation margins
- Fintechs tackling opportunities arising from the disaggregation of previously aggregated tasks

The first two of these, monetary TxCs earned by banks and intermediation margins, are covered in the remainder of this section. In technique K, following this section, we will delve into the smorgasbord of impending opportunities that will arise out of the disaggregation of the various tasks undertaken by these institutions.

Fintechs Going After Monetary TxCs Earned by Banks

Not surprisingly, high-profile monetary TxCs were the first place for banks to be put under pressure. It is hard to see how a bank will sustain monetary TxCs; with ever-increasing automation, the marginal cost of a banking transaction trends toward zero. Yet monetary charges are widespread. Merchants that take credit cards pay a small percentage on those credit card sales. Consumers and corporates pay a percentage on their foreign exchange (FX) transactions. Stockbroking firms charge per transaction. Insurance brokers charge fees on policy issuance. Real estate brokers in the United States take 4 to 6 percent of the sale price.

Spreads and commissions on retail cash FX transactions can be greater than 7 percent. Admittedly, the handling of cash adds more complexity beyond the simple exchange process. If done electronically (not involving the use of cash) the monetary charge might be 1 to 2 percent. For large companies the spread might be five basis points (0.05 percent). A neutral observer might not unreasonably expect that over time, the rates paid by consumers might gravitate toward the level of those of large companies.

The point is not just the saving of the commission or spread on the existing transactions. As monetary charges fall, the number of exchanges has the potential to multiply. More exchanges potentially lead to vast value pools and enhanced happiness. Consider international remittances from migrants in wealthy countries back to their families in less prosperous countries. The charges for these sorts of services are high and people are working on myriad approaches for getting the money from the sender to the receiver, who might be living in a village with no formal banking or even cell phones. Eventually, this will become a frictionless transaction and the volumes flowing will multiply.

One might think that at five basis points for a FX transaction for a large company that the TxC-reduction game is over. There surely can't be much more of a prize to capture. Perhaps in the future, people will be appalled by the fact that spreads of five basis points were in place, especially since the marginal cost of a FX transaction is only a tiny fraction of five basis points (as opposed to the average cost of such a transaction—taking into account all the systems put in place by players in the sector). At some level the concept of transaction fees on payments is somewhat anathema—if I handed another person a $20 bill in fulfilment of some owed money (e.g., a lunch), if a third party decided to take 0.5 percent of it, I would be appalled. In the coming digital world, money and value transfer will merely be an uptick and a downtick on a ledger.

Fintechs Working to Compete Away Intermediation Margins

The most important part of a traditional bank has been its role as an intermediary, particularly as a lender. Lending is often seen as the essential task of a bank.

In practice, the bank provides an intermediation service between two proprietary swarms—a swarm of borrowers and a swarm of lenders (depositors). While the borrowers pay interest to the bank, they are not really giving the interest to the bank.

The bank is a go-between in the middle of the borrowers and depositors. This has been a very useful service for borrowers as, if the borrower had to go out and find a bunch of depositors to lend it money for an agreed period and pull together a contract to govern the relationship, the vast majority of borrowing and lending transactions would not happen due to the TxCs. These TxCs are not wildly different from the TxCs we saw in relation to borrowing a hedge trimmer from someone in my neighborhood.

To reward the bank for the important role it has played in reducing TxCs between savers and borrowers, banks have typically earned about 3 percent as measured by the typical net interest margin (NIM) of banks. Simplified, the net interest margin is the blended rate that the bank charges borrowers less the blended rate it pays to depositors for holding their money. This is their income on loans and deposits.

This income of roughly 3 percent to the bank covers three broad areas:

1. Overheads associated with managing the borrowers and depositors—setting up the transactions, assessing the creditworthiness of the borrower, running the systems, monitoring performance of the borrower, etc.
2. Absorbing credit losses in the event that some of the borrowers do not pay their loans back
3. Profit for the bank

While banks have varying cost-to-income ratios (roughly, overheads as a percentage of net interest margin and fees), 66 percent would not be unusual. Looking at things extremely simplistically, overheads normally absorb two-thirds of the 3 percentage points of the income margin of the bank, leaving 1 percent of the value of the loans outstanding to cover credit losses (which banks don't explicitly charge depositors for) and profit for the bank, let's say 0.5 percent for credit losses and 0.5 percent for profit.

There are several swarm (peer-to-peer) fintech players focused on reducing the TxCs of the traditional banking intermediation model and passing on the savings to savers and borrowers through better rates. Some fintechs are focused on gathering deposits from consumers and lending to other consumers; others are gathering deposits from consumers and lending to small businesses. There is no reason why these peer-to-peer players will not extend to the full customer range of small consumers to large corporates on both the borrowing and lending side of the transactions. The highest current intermediation percentages are paid by consumers and small businesses, so entrepreneurs are logically focused there first. Putting aside the credit losses, the new swarm players have a cost envelope of 2.5 percent to work within (the 2 percent allocated to overhead and the 0.5 percent in profit); sadly, credit losses will always be with us. When building their businesses, the swarm players may have unattractive average cost bases, but once the swarm is up and running, the marginal cost economics will take over. The cost to acquire customers will be high up front but should decrease rapidly over time.

Trust will be a big factor in the early success of these intermediation fintechs. Lack of trust leads to high customer acquisition costs early on, but as depositors begin receiving good returns on their deposits, trust will grow and becomes less of a concern.

Other than tackling the 2.5 percent cost envelope, the best fintechs are doing the same as the other TxC crushers such as Uber and Airbnb. They are systematically eliminating the barriers that customers might have to using them. For example, the user-friendliness of the platforms of the fintechs for lending and borrowing money tends to be much better than that of the incumbent banks. Big institutions tend to be sluggish on the innovation front. While there is no theoretical reason why the loan application process from a traditional bank should not be as appealing to consumers as that from one of these new intermediation platforms, the new platforms are nimbler, with a relentless focus on speeding up and simplifying the process, and crushing TxCs.

○ ○ ○

In this section we looked at how monetary TxCs and intermediation margins are likely to fall as they are targeted by new, largely disaggregated players. In technique K, we will look disaggregation of tasks in a banking context.

TECHNIQUE K:
DISAGGREGATING TASKS

Disaggregation is a never-ending journey leading to more refined specialization and continual release of new pools of value. An entrepreneur who applies foresight to the process of disaggregation can look at the existing tasks currently undertaken by every company and take a view as to whether there is an opportunity to take one of those tasks out of the company, do it better than it is done today, and turn it into a stand-alone business. In this technique we will take a typical aggregated bank as our target for disaggregation and see what opportunities might arise.

An Aggregated Bank

Banks are among the most persistently aggregated businesses that we encounter in the world. The breadth of product offerings is outstanding. Thought of as a series of product groups, an aggregated bank typically encompasses:

* Mortgages
* Payments
* Foreign exchange
* Savings and deposits
* Investments
* Credit cards
* Personal loans
* Asset finance
* Car leasing
* Small business loans
* Treasury
* Corporate lending
* Trade finance

The complexity of managing these different groups within a bank's hierarchy would test anyone's managerial and coordination skills. Banks do their best to inject some market-like processes, such as allocating capital and setting internal transfer prices, on the capital allocated to each business unit. But none of these processes can replicate the powerful signals that true prices can convey in a world of exchange based on markets.

Banks tend to dress up the breadth of the product offering as a one-stop-shop benefit to their customers. In practice, the existence of multiple product groups in a bank (with segregated income statements and different goals) addressing the same customers leads to inevitable conflicts. For example, the deposit-taking side of the bank might be trying to shed deposits (when interest rates are low or negative), thereby antagonizing large corporate customers, at the same that the lending side of the bank is trying to sell loans to them.

Disaggregation into Product Groups

The most obvious first line of investigation for any budding entrepreneur wanting to disaggregate a bank is to consider whether he or she could do a better job at one of the product groups than the bank—maybe with some sort of new twist in the value proposition. Set up a mortgage-only business with a dedicated funding source such as a life insurance company that likes long-term, fixed-rate mortgage assets? A new investment platform for people in the middle of the assets pyramid, as opposed to those at the top who are pursued by virtually all wealth management companies? A new car leasing business aimed primarily at gig economy drivers?

Disaggregation into product groups is already well underway across different jurisdictions. The product groups of most banks already have single-product specialist competitors. While that doesn't mean there is no opportunity for fresh-faced entrepreneurs, at this point most tf the opportunity for disaggregation at a product group level is well signaled. Prospective entrepreneurs are always better off pressing their ears against the train track to figure out what is coming soon.

In banking it is extremely hard to have differentiation at the product level. One bank's innovative mortgage product can be copied very quickly by other players in the sector. Indeed, the ability for a bank to launch new products (mortgages, saving, leasing) is normally limited by the flexibility of the bank's software architecture.

Disaggregation to the Next Level Below Product Groups

While the opportunity for entrepreneurship is always possible at the product group level, maybe it is worth looking one level lower. To pick one of the product groups to explore disaggregating further, let's look at mortgages.

The first place to start is by identifying the subtasks in the mortgage-granting process. These steps (and substeps) include:

- Attract potential mortgage customers to your bank (place advertising, build relationships with estate agents, undertake digital marketing, etc.).
- Provide preliminary mortgage approval (gather basic data on income, assess likely deposit, calculate the maximum likely mortgage, grant preliminary approval, etc.).
- Undertake due diligence (perform legal check to ensure there is no existing mortgage on the house, check the prospective borrower's credit in credit bureaus, do independent valuation of the house and review its structural assessment, etc.).
- Validate, mathematically, the ability of the borrower to make repayments (review recent pay stubs, check bank statements [multiple accounts perhaps] to develop a view on the actual level of free cash flow likely available, check the house deposit, etc.).
- Check people's identity (know your customer).
- Run algorithms and credit scorecard to determine if applicant is a good risk.
- Prepare mortgage document (get the house deeds, etc.).
- Service the mortgage over time (collect payments, ensure paperwork is in order, chase late payments, etc.).

It is an endless series of tasks, or so it seems to the borrower, never mind the poor unfortunate mortgage processing staff. All of these tasks, bundled up into a bank's hierarchy today, are prospective individual business opportunities for an entrepreneur. As TxCs for coordinating tasks across companies fall, and as entrepreneurs figure out how to turn these tasks into specialized on-demand services, the glue that binds them into the hierarchy starts to loosen.

In fact, for the bank, virtually all the tasks involved in something like the mortgage process are simply chores that need to be executed efficiently on the path to the real revenue event—the granting of the mortgage. If you asked the bank if it aspired to be world-class at all these tasks, its response would probably be that it is just trying to be good enough and reasonably cost efficient at getting the task done. Given the diversity of the tasks, it would be nonsense to aim to be world-class across many of them. Most tasks are done in-house because it would involve too many TxCs to plug in a third party to undertake them. Others are kept in-house because the bank considers them to be strategic or sensitive (or core competences, to use the corporate strategy phrase). For example, if the bank had spent years or even decades building up special relationships with real estate brokers to get leads on prospective home buyers, outsourcing that task probably makes less sense, as those relationships might give the bank an advantage in the market.

Why Go Deeper in Disaggregation?

The more an entrepreneur disaggregates, the more she has a chance of unearthing a subtask where she can do something special and create a defensible position versus competitors. This special something might involve achieving a much lower cost per task undertaken. It could mean a higher level of skill and professionalism. It could be that the time taken to undertake the task can be sped up. Remember: the first goal is to eliminate the TxCs to the bank and make it a truly on-demand service. The fact that the task is now undertaken by a third party should be almost imperceptible.

What about the concern that Adam Smith raised? It is fine to specialize (disaggregate more deeply), but eventually one runs up against the limitation of the size of the market, beyond which it is not worth specializing. This is where perhaps the corporate strategist will diverge from the economists. Developing a business is not a linear activity whereby one sets a goal and a series of tasks to get there, and then undertakes this series of tasks in an unthinking manner, on a critical path to the prize. Developing a business is an exercise in starting to pursue a business plan and, just by taking some early steps, opening a series of real options over time. The entrepreneur might start out in the pin-making business and, lo and behold, spot a new opportunity that has opened in the paper clip sector because of the skills and knowledge gained in making pins.

All this is to say that deciding to pursue a disaggregated entrepreneurial opportunity that on the surface might seem to have a small addressable market often leads to new larger opportunities further down the road. The real goal of the disaggregating entrepreneur is to develop superior capability in a task that can be offered to all players in the sector (e.g., all banks), across multiple geographies, and, hopefully, across other sectors and use cases that had not been originally envisaged.

Disaggregating Even Deeper into Mortgage Processing

To explore the possibilities that emerge as an entrepreneur goes deeper, I have picked one subtask of the mortgage processing business system—checking people's identity and performing *know your customer* (KYC) on the applicant.

This by itself might entail a few tasks such as:

* Getting a copy of the borrower's driver's license or passport
* Asking for two utility bills
* Performing checks and validations on the documents

These are modest, mundane tasks. By the time the bank asks for these documents, sends them to the mortgage processing center, enters them in some system by scanning or some other process, performs some validation tests on them (or simply looks at them), and someone checks a few boxes, the bank has incurred a reasonable amount of cost, which is buried in the general mortgage cost center base.

No one is expecting a bank to become world-class at these microtasks. The best they hope for is that they are not too inefficient at them—the volume of activity going through these processes will normally be subscale.

Let's look at it from the perspective of the entrepreneur. The entrepreneur might become enamored with the opportunity to build a world-class "checker of passports" business. What does "deliver a world-class passport checking" task mean? I suspect that it might involve some of the following:

* Knowing the layout of passports from all 200-odd countries in the world
* Knowing the layout of every iteration of passport that they have issued over the past 10 years
* Knowing which passport numbers are valid
* Checking that the signature matches the printed name on the passport application
* Estimating the age of the person in the photo and using it to cross-check the stated age
* Testing any built-in holograms and security devices
* Ensuring the passport date is still valid
* Doing an online search to see if there are any outstanding legal issues against the applicant

Clearly the bank has no chance of doing all these microtasks to a world-class standard and, probably, no desire to do them. They will be subscale in their operations; these are chores and are not at all strategic to the bank. Why shouldn't the bank be availing of an on-demand service? Indeed, why wouldn't the bank preemptively disaggregate by actively encouraging budding entrepreneurs to come in to review the bank's less vital processes and tasks to put together a world-class on-demand service?

A focused entrepreneur has the chance of mastering all these tasks to become a world expert in passport checking. With the world moving toward on-demand services where a company can plug in and consume as much of the service as it needs, it is conceivable that an entrepreneur can make this into a business.

The entrepreneur might turn to the bank and offer to check passports for 10 cents each or $1 each, depending on volume, with an on-demand response time of one-hundredth of a second. Maybe it becomes a multilayered service, whereby a basic passport check costs 5 cents, and an intensive search costs $5.

One of the most interesting things about disaggregating business processes to such a low level is that one suddenly starts to see that basic elemental tasks, such as checking the passport, are extensible into many other areas, showing up in all sorts of places. Passport checking can be done for other mortgage companies, passport checking when you buy a mobile phone, passport checking at the airport, passport checking for registering a company, passport checking when one picks up prescription drugs, passport checking for transferring foreign currency, or passport checking for opening an account.

In fact, the better and more cheaply the entrepreneur can deliver the service, the more it opens possibilities for exchange—more reasons to check passports. Maybe if credit card losses spike in a tourist center, the retailers might start checking passports (because now it is simple and inexpensive). Lower TxCs open the sluice gates to more exchange, and to more diverse and exciting reasons to exchange.

Adam Smith's concerns about the size of the market—that, as one specializes, one could end up with smaller and smaller opportunities—turns out to be only a theoretical concern. The smart entrepreneur can offer his or her low-TxC service to all sorts of applications across multiple sectors.

Even Further Disaggregation . . .

Thorough checking of passports requires a smorgasbord of capabilities—photo analysis, hologram testing, fingerprint analysis, and similarity of data matching that require distinct deep technical expertise. One great thing about the world of falling TxCs is that all of these potential further disaggregated services can themselves be procured on an on-demand basis. In fact, the smart entrepreneur might be the one who procures all the underlying tasks on an on-demand basis from different providers, and then simply reaggregates them into one firehose of passport-checking tasks for those who want it.

Even though it feels like we have lowered TxCs and opened a new value pool of passport checking and that's that, all that has happened is that the nirvana of zero TxC has receded further into the horizon. The process of disaggregating (and reaggregating)—the cycle of innovation—begins again and new value pools emerge; happiness increases.

CHAPTER 18

TxCs and Disaggregation in Universities

I n the previous chapter we covered the ways in which tasks in a bank could be disaggregated. In this chapter we do the same for universities.

The university is one of the most fascinating industry sectors to examine. It has been almost frozen in time for 500-plus years as an aggregated unit. A professor in ancient Roman history from the year 1650 would slot seamlessly into the classroom of today and would, no doubt, be much sought after in any university for his or her unique perspectives. Little has changed; PowerPoint might befuddle him, like it does the rest of us.

The economic forces of specialization and consequent productivity improvement that flow through all business institutions via the pressures of competition in the market have scarcely touched the university sector. The brand-name universities of today are, in large part, the brand-name universities of centuries gone by. It is hard to think of brands in any other sector that have had such longevity. The changes that could have reshaped the sector have been held back through the inherit conservatism and rigid labor structures of the institutions, largely paid for by national governments, creating local monopolies. These TxCs have clogged up productivity improvement in the sector, and we now have a heavily overengineered university sector with a vast hierarchy that costs much more than it should—whether it is paid for by the students or the taxpayers around them.

These powerful (and largely self-imposed) TxCs create a metaphorical ocean of value that is just waiting to be unleashed in the university sector. This makes the sector an excellent case study to use for looking at falling (and fallen) TxCs, speculating the shape of the university of tomorrow, and identifying entrepreneurial opportunities that might yield value over the next 5 to 10 years.

THE PURPOSE OF A UNIVERSITY

On entering "the role of a university?" into a search engine, one comes up with a remarkable array of answers, from "repositories and generators of knowledge," to "discover and invent the future," to "leaders in teaching and learning," and "teaching students how to think." Rarely is mentioned the more prosaic role of teaching students what they need to know in their chosen fields. History students learn from the past; engineers learn how to construct buildings that won't collapse; business students learn how to understand a balance sheet. Perhaps that ambiguity in purpose contributes to the bloating in the cost and functions of a modern university.

For our purposes, let's assume that the sole role of the university is its more prosaic role—that of teaching students what they need to know in their chosen field. Looking at the university through this teaching lens, on the one hand we have a swarm of lecturers with knowledge and teaching skills (we will include all the gradations of lecturers including professors and teaching assistants). These lecturers mainly exist within the hierarchy of the university and, in large part, are coordinated by the university infrastructure. Some of the lecturers have very tenuous links to the college and their employment is very loose; this is more to suit the university than to suit the lecturer, as most lecturers want to get the benefits of permanency available to the higher grades of professor. They are not disaggregated from the university by choice. They have little or no direct access to the market (students hungry to learn) except through the hierarchy. Some of the insider lecturers face the same low power dynamics that the outside lecturers face.

On the other hand, we have a cadre of students who desire to gain knowledge and insight—whether for career-oriented purposes or just because the subject interests them. They want good lecturers, good grades, and a valued degree.

At its simplest, the university mediates between two swarms—matching lecturers and students (like Uber's drivers and riders). For good measure, the university injects trust into the process. Not only are the universities accredited for granting degrees, but students and employers are aware of the relative reputational value of different institutions. If the student gets a degree in bridge building from a university known for a good engineering program, that indicates quality.

THE ACTIVITIES THAT MAKE UP A UNIVERSITY

The university is a very highly aggregated entity. The campuses are typically vast—almost like a cloistered world. They house, feed, teach, and socialize their students.

The major tasks can be summarized as:

* Student recruitment
* Program and curriculum policy and development
* Student management
* University management
* Buildings and lecture halls
* Study rooms
* Library services
* Lecturing
* Professor and lecturer management
* Grading and assessment
* Support and ancillary services
* Degree granting

Like the banking example, each of these major tasks could be broken down into successively smaller tasks until one gets to microtasks at the end of the tree. Micro they may be, but they can still be mission critical.

WHICH TASKS COULD BE DISAGGREGATED?

As one goes down through the list of all these tasks, opportunities to specialize jump out on all fronts. You get the distinct feeling that if you took any university task and specialized in it, you could probably do it much better than most universities could by themselves. For example, take the task of program and course development. Most lecturers today do this largely in a vacuum without any real training as to how to put together a world-class course or an entire program. Someone with global expertise in this task would add a lot of value to many universities in the world.

Every task could be disaggregated. As well as doing a better job if tasks were specialized, all the tasks could probably be disaggregated without a lot of bother. In fact, when looking at the list of tasks that comprise a university on an individual basis, virtually all look very mundane, and it is hard to get excited or worried if they were not to be "inside" the university. For example:

- **Student recruitment.** In many cases the search for overseas students is already passed to a specialist third party.
- **Grading and assessment.** Grading and assessment are thorns in the side of lecturers. Long hours grading and perennially unhappy students may make lecturers happy for a third party to conduct this activity.
- **Library.** Could this be as easy to disaggregate as food services?

If we looked at the university's major tasks at the microtask level, we would find the tasks even easier to disaggregate. The institution still has the essence of a university if it outsources student recruitment or gets an outside specialist program design company to craft its degree programs. There is no sense that one has damaged the core mission—that of teaching students.

Perhaps the only one activity that a university would consider to be its crown jewel (and that must be kept inside the institution) is the degree-granting authority of the university; that feels like the soul of the institution. Without that, what is it? Could it still consider itself a real university if it outsourced degree granting?

Perhaps degree granting might be disaggregated if a top 10 global university were to be willing to grant degrees to the students of a humble local university (due to the quality of the underlying program). Would the students of such a humble university not be glad to receive such a higher ranked degree? The president of the humble university might not agree, as he or she might feel relegated to the role of a branch manager, rather than occupying the locally exalted role of university president.

After looking at the tasks one by one, most universities can be described as vertically integrated entities that could be disaggregated into their constituent parts, allowing specialization to work its magic. A university could become a virtual entity (with degree-granting authority or not) that is held together with a strong set of legal contracts.

TxCS THAT HOLD THE UNIVERSITY TOGETHER

Consequently, with a clear benefit to specialization across most of the tasks that a university undertakes and with disaggregation also possible for each of the individual tasks that a university carries out, the only thing holding it together in its fully aggregated state is TxCs. The primary TxC for most universities is the privileged position that they have as local, subsidized monopolies and oligopolies. Students in a region or country are largely stuck with the universities close to them—it is the tyranny of geography, backed up by governmental protection for their privileged positions. Furthermore, branded universities have the protection of their brand names and massive excess demand by students for places in their hallowed cloisters.

These TxC protections and privileged positions mean that universities do not have to let the economic forces of specialization and consequent disaggregation work their effect on productivity in the sector. The institutions are calcified.

WHY THIS IS CHANGING NOW

The TxC of geography is changing; the world is opening up in front of students. A major TxC that students faced was the need to exchange with their lecturers through the medium of classrooms in a physical campus. This result in local oligopolies—enrollments and class sizes were determined by the size of lecture halls and seats in labs.

Prior to the arrival of Covid-19, online learning was the much-talked-about coming wave that hadn't quite come ashore. Many universities or individual lecturers had dabbled with online courses—many free. Portions of courses delivered in person were uploaded to the internet. It would be fair to say that online learning was seen as the poor relation of the high-quality, high-cost traditional university. Employers discounted online learning without even consciously thinking about it.

Necessity being the motherhood of invention, online learning took off in March 2020, and it isn't looking back. Clearly, there are still problems with the quality of the online learning experience—the technology can be clunky, lecturers are still evolving their teaching styles to suit the new medium, and students are missing out on the all-embracing experience of campus life. These are solvable problems.

Let's stick with the fundamental exchange going on in the university; the student exchanging with lecturers to gain knowledge. This no longer occurs solely through the classroom in a physical campus. We have had a dramatic fall in TxCs due to the inroads of online learning arising from the pandemic. The fall in TxCs is happening on very fertile ground—the universities are not ready for competition from specialized, disaggregated providers.

Who knows when the full impact of this new world will hit? Students and governments might continue to be willing to pay for the high-cost service they get today. But the new models for delivery will mean that the foundations of the local university monopoly will become less stable over time. At the same time as the geography TxC is falling, we have a number of accelerators kicking in, such as the idle inventory of lecturer capacity, powerful marginal cost dynamics, and the ability to create a swarm.

There is an enormous excess supply ("idle inventory") of lecturers in the world. The sector has many mechanisms for separating insiders from outsiders, with the primary goal of restricting supply. People need PhDs; a multitiered system of professors keeps the supply and the spoils tight. This means there is an underutilized and under-rewarded cadre of willing lecturers. Furthermore, online teaching means a multiplication of the potential supply. A world-class lecturer (with her own brand or cachet in her subject area) in some branch of artificial intelligence (AI) who sits in California, London, or Shanghai can move from teaching a maximum of, say, 150 students in a class to thousands (subject of course to the TxCs associated with such a vast array of students). Lecturers are no longer hidebound by the tyranny of geography. There is a wave of teaching capacity about to be unleashed on the market.

The marginal cost economics in the field of education are incredibly appealing. The average cost to deliver a teaching capability through a traditional university is extremely high. Buildings, student accommodation, staff with low teaching hours, etc. all need to be paid for by the students (or their governments). It is subject to average cost economics. Getting this average cost down would be very challenging without dramatically changing the product—university fees and costs to students have only increased over time. It is an average cost aimed at the very top of the pyramid—relatively affluent students in well-to-do countries. Online is a marginal cost world, as the cost of one additional student is almost zero. One great lecturer can, in theory, teach every single person in the world at almost zero marginal cost. Lecturers aiming to supplement their income through online teaching will be able to offer their services on a marginal cost basis.

The field of education offers great potential for creating swarms. Most exchanges in the world of teaching involve the student contracting with the university, due to the effective market power of the public universities (and brand name private universities). If students were sophisticated consumers of university-level education, they would be exchanging directly with the relevant lecturers (or roster of lecturers) through some sort of marketplace. This would be the perfect model, as it would give a lot of flexibility (and lower TxCs) to the students.

There will be dramatic winners and losers in this marketplace—the AI lecturer with her own brand in the market will likely be a winner. A lecturer without any distinctive subject matter expertise in a local university that previously had an effective monopoly over the demand of local students will be a loser. This is not meant to be a value judgment on the merits of different types of university experiences—it is trying to demonstrate how, eventually, the fundamental economics are likely to play out. Local universities are not going to have local oligopolies over the best (or indeed any) of the local students. The swarm of students is likely to meet the swarm of lecturers directly at some stage, without the need for the university providing a very expensive mediation service in the middle—in the same way that banks are unlikely to maintain their current mediation role between borrowers and savers without adapting to the new world.

The early signs of such a teaching swarm meeting a student swarm can be seen in online language learning, where one can exchange with qualified teachers and "community" teachers with all the variety of offering that one might expect. What accent do I want to learn? Taught by a man or woman? From my favorite city in France? Well rated and reviewed by the community? Discussing business, politics, or sports?

The goal here is not to crystal-ball the future of the university industry. However, it might be the most fascinating example of TxCs collapsing before our eyes, turbocharged by the high average cost structures of existing players that can be supplanted by marginal cost players and large quantities of idle lecturing inventory that should be able to be harnessed in a marketplace.

CHAPTER 19

Reaggregations, Swarms, and Virtualized Firms

F irst, let's recap. In a world of zero TxCs, there would be no hierarchies. Individual disaggregated tasks would be done by different firms. Every task would be coordinated and choreographed perfectly in an on-demand, completely disaggregated manner. We would have incredibly deep specialization and division of labor. The productivity levels would be extraordinary.

Such a world is still at the horizon—infinite years away. The designers of organizations need to live in the mundane here and now of lingering TxCs. What are the possible waystations from today's world of relatively aggregated firms to the horizon of completely disaggregated firms? What will be the impact of falling TxCs on the architecture of our corporations? These are important questions for entrepreneurs.

PUTTING THE BUILDING BLOCKS TOGETHER AGAIN

Full disaggregation is the feeling a child gets when he or she gets the big new box of building blocks with none of them stuck together. The possibilities are limitless: tractors, airports, castles, cranes. Our ability to put the pieces together is limited only by our own creativity.

Disaggregation allows the organization designer to think about how to put together tasks from scratch. Those that are mission critical can be kept inside the firm, and those that are not central to the mission and would benefit by specialization by a third party can be passed to an entrepreneur.

THE ENTREPRENEUR AS ARCHITECT

Once the entrepreneur has listed out all the tasks and micro-tasks in a sector or specific company, the entrepreneur is now the architect who can pick up all the individual tasks, look at them, and see if there are interesting new ways of putting them together—in theory as simple as snapping together some building blocks. The architect should be considering and testing the boundaries of the firm constantly and asking questions such as:

- What tasks does the firm currently perform that might be candidates to pass to a third party (disaggregation)?
- Would disaggregation yield an opportunity for specialization with consequential benefits for the party passing the task to the third party, and not just the entrepreneur?
- For each of these tasks, do TxCs (lack of trust, worries about being taken advantage of, potential stranded assets, etc.) inhibit the firm from disaggregating them? How much further do TxCs need to fall before disaggregation could be considered as a realistic option?
- Which specific tasks does the architect believe deliver the essence of the company's value proposition? Is it as narrow as one or two of the tasks?
- If the firm was to map out the potential disaggregation of its tasks and have the luxury of choosing which ones to keep within the firm (e.g., due to importance to the mission of the firm), which ones would it keep versus which ones would it pass on?

Rarely does a firm have someone whose job is to think about these issues explicitly. What tends to happen is that large firms get into periodic bouts of urgent and immediate cost reduction (e.g., due to a general recession driving a need for belt-tightening), and only then does it start to think about the boundaries of the firm. In such a frenzy, it looks at boundaries mainly through a cost reduction outsourcing lens—"How much can we save right now?"—not through a strategic consideration as to what should be in the firm and what should be out.

o o o

The advantage of viewing the firm as a disaggregated list of tasks, like a box of building blocks, is that the designer of the firm has a repertoire of possible configurations at his or her fingertips.

HORIZONTAL REAGGREGATION

With falling TxCs, the ability to coordinate across firms increases and the need to hold tasks tight within the hierarchy declines. As these tasks come loose from the hierarchy, it is perhaps inevitable that the same tasks in different companies (e.g., passport checking within a bank) will come together in the interest of scale and skills—if one bank is subscale in passport checking, then most or all of them probably are.

It could be that one bank decides to do a rollup of the disaggregated passport-checking operations of many banks, or maybe a new player comes along with a specialized, highly performant, on-demand process to coax all the banks to use its service. Either way, horizontal integration of tasks (as shown in Figure 19.1) across multiple banks is the outcome.

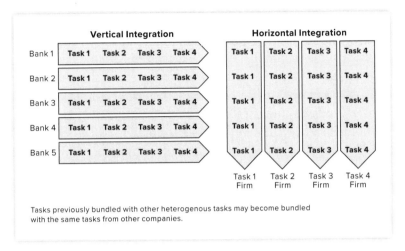

Figure 19.1 Moving from Vertical Integration to Horizontal Integration

SWARMS

We discussed swarms in earlier chapters. The concept of a swarm is not something completely new—there have been swarms of taxi drivers in every city in the world for many decades. What is different now is that the swarms starting to arrive across many sectors can be integrated through online software platforms and bolstered by technologies such as GPS to deliver an on-demand customer service that simply wasn't possible in the past.

The productivity benefits of running a service through a (maybe self-managing) swarm will far outweigh those of keeping people working together through a hierarchy. Swarms could be groups of lenders or borrowers for personal or small business or even corporate loans. They could be groups of hosts who own holiday rental apartments around the world, or groups of people who want to rent holiday apartments. They could be a group of accountants who form together under the banner of Certified Public Accountants or Chartered Accountants. They could be groups of plumbers that suffer from lack of client *trust* and desire to become part of a swarm to reduce the TxC of trust. They could be restaurants that suffered from the *inability of consumers to search the market* and join the swarm of restaurants on the restaurant ordering app. They could be delivery drivers who have no way of finding restaurants who need drivers tonight.

In fact, a swarm is possible and probably suitable any time we have individuals or small firms that suffer badly from TxCs such as *lack of ability to search the market* (they can't be found), *trust*, or *challenges in contracting*. As we move toward a disaggregated world, we will have many more people and small firms that are entrepreneurial sole traders. Joining a swarm gives them the ability to solve many of the issues that inhibit them from exchanging with customers. Swarms exist to crush TxCs.

Networks become stronger and more valuable with each node that is added to the network. For Uber, each driver added to the network boosts the value of the network. Having more drivers means shorter wait times, and the gains from shorter wait times are valuable to people looking for a ride; it starts to feel increasingly like a true on-demand service.

In the era in which we live, we need someone to provide the entrepreneurial spark to create a swarm where one doesn't exist before. As you can see in the stock market valuations of some of the swarm companies (Etsy, eBay, Upwork, Uber, Airbnb), the ringmasters of the swarm are able to establish themselves in a powerful and valuable position, solely through their ability to crush TxCs.

In a fluid world where the inhibitors to exchange are always falling, business models that make sense today can be quickly washed away by other models with lower TxCs. The branded swarms of today that are emerging across the landscape of small businesses will hopefully become open source and completely self-managing over time. The branded swarms have powerful positions today, but swarm members may aim to take back that power over time.

VIRTUALIZED FIRMS

In a world where everything is heading toward on-demand and every task can be plugged together seamlessly, it is hard, in the long run, to see there being an entrepreneurial opportunity in being a virtualized aggregator of tasks carried out by others, without adding some value in the process. But we live in a world of imperfection and still declining TxCs—there is still room for partially aggregated firms.

In the example of passport checking, we saw the types of detailed checks (disaggregated tasks) that might possibly be carried out on a passport, including photo analysis, hologram testing, fingerprint analysis, and similarity of data matching. An entrepreneur might look at this situation and come up with a virtual proposition that pulls together all these checks into one integrated service that he or she offers on-demand to banks, border police, and other passport checkers. This could be a virtualized firm—absolutely everything outsourced—virtually virtualized!

Let's return to our broader set of mortgage processes. At any point across the broad process, the bank might decide that it wants a strategic partner who would pull together many of the disaggregated processes into a virtualized single offering. For example, there is a wide set of tasks around the issue of creditworthiness. Does the customer have sufficient income? Is he or she a wasteful spender, based on an analytical review of bank accounts? What information is available from the credit bureau, and how should it be interpreted? There is a long list of information gathering and sifting tasks that go into forming a view as to whether a particular person should get a mortgage. The bank might decide that its real intellectual property is the credit algorithms rather than the data gathering, and maybe it makes sense for it to have one partner to orchestrate all the data gathering and sifting subprocesses done by various disaggregated task-based firms. Of course, down the road, as TxCs fall further and when the bank is ready, it might decide that it is ready to deal with disaggregated services directly and so cut out the intermediation cost of the virtualized player.

PARTIALLY REAGGREGATED FIRMS

Over the medium term, partially reaggregated firms are the form that we will see most frequently. Of the 20 or so major tasks involved to deliver a mortgage, the mortgage business architect might decide that only two of them need to be kept in-house, for reasons of competitive advantage. These two might be (1) relationships with real estate agents who will direct leads to the mortgage company, and (2) developing credit scoring algorithms to ensure that the mortgage company only takes on the best risks. The architect might decide to reaggregate these two tasks and to outsource all the other tasks to third parties.

More companies are going to face these sorts of architecture decisions. They will not be able to compete with specialized disaggregated processes on a task-by-task basis. Disaggregation of tasks down to the core few is the tough execution path facing an incumbent player like an existing bank. The lucky new entrant starts from a different place. Maybe it might decide to focus on one task and achieve excellence in it through specialization. It might also group some tasks together, some of which it does itself and some of which are outsourced. For example, a new entrant into the mortgage processing space might decide to be the "house" expert—setting up and checking structural assessments, getting and checking the formal house documents, undertaking a valuation and assessing the agreed price for the house versus the valuation, and handling and storing mortgage documents. In doing so, it would be creating a partially reaggregated offering.

The point of examining this detail is to show that it is unlikely there will be vertically integrated mortgage businesses in the future. There will be businesses with a single-minded focus on one task—maybe customer gathering, house valuation checking, income evaluation for mortgage suitability, or algorithm specialist. Maybe they will focus on several tasks that fit together very naturally.

TECHNIQUE L:
REAGGREGATING TASKS

Let's reconsider the university as a target for reaggregation. How might the disaggregated tasks that are done in a university fit back together to deliver innovative propositions?

Universities operate in a sector that has skated past the forces of specialization and disaggregation. In economic terms, it has not scaled, and in its current form it is not scalable—the "chalk and talk" model with a lecturer at the front of the class is often only effective for class sizes of fewer than one or two hundred students. Without a scalable working model, the annualized cost per student—whether at a private or public university—has well outstripped the general rate of inflation.

Most students are ignorant consumers of university-level education. They suffer from the TxCs: students struggle to search across the market; universities in most countries are geographically focused; students don't have any sense of which lecturers are world-class and which ones are not; students rely on very limited data points to form views on their preferred courses; governments subsidize the product heavily and in a relatively undifferentiating manner (capacity for student numbers is more important than quality, in most cases). In summary, there is very poor matching between the supply of courses and the demand from students. Except for highly ranked, branded universities, it is unclear whether the universities would (and should) attract sufficient student demand without the huge subsidies applied to keep fees low enough.

The effect of TxCs can be seen easily in the European Union. Even though it is very slowly becoming one large market for education, and though the European Union wants to promote mobility within Europe, the percentage of students that go overseas for their undergraduate degrees is still low. Better information, easier application processes, recommendations from former students, and more discerning employers—all good TxC reductions—will solve this lack of exchange in the coming decade. As will the free or very low-cost degree programs now available from well-ranked European universities!

In addition to the high TxCs, universities everywhere are still extremely highly aggregated institutions—nearly all their tasks are conducted in-house. With the number of TxCs leading to poor matching of supply and demand, and high levels of aggregation, the university sector is surely ripe for disaggregation and consequently is ready for the reaggregation of tasks in exciting ways to create new business models.

○ ○ ○

I don't have any unique insights to the university of the future—I am only harnessing the power of specialization and relaxing the current TxCs to see what might be possible. Let's do some disaggregating and reaggregating and start pulling potential future university business models and opportunities out of the air!

Let's Create a New University!

Creating a new university is probably not the best business idea an entrepreneur has come up with, but let's explore how it might be possible. As a smart entrepreneur (and a committed disaggregationist!), your thinking will probably pursue the following lines:

- I need a great product or service proposition that will wow a reasonably well-sized segment of the student population.
- I want to do only the minimum number of tasks necessary to get this product to market.
- I have very little capital, so I want to do this on a shoestring. Preferably it will be mainly self-funding.

You will likely end up focusing on subject areas where student demand is high—let's pick artificial intelligence (AI), which is the technology fad du jour of the early 2020s. You start by signing up several good AI lecturers in a pay-per-course gig economy mode. You decide to go fully online, or maybe lease a premises (preferably just for the school term every year). You need accreditation, but maybe in the short run you decide to utilize and pay for the degree-granting capability of an existing cash-poor university—you find one with a good name that would value the income. You use a student recruitment firm that is paid for every seat filled on the course. You pay a student placement firm to place the students with major firms interested in hiring good AI graduates; maybe the companies might even pay part (or all) of a student's fees for the course up front if the student commits to working for the firm. You scroll down through the list of tasks that need to be done, and you find a firm that is best-in-class at each of them.

This is all not completely implausible—in fact, it feels quite doable. What you have managed to do is to create an on-demand university by snapping together the building blocks of tasks undertaken by third parties. You are generating income and cash flow from day one (if the students and companies pay up front). You have avoided the need for capital expenditure of any significance. Someone working from their home office could, in theory, conjure up this university out of thin air with an integrated set of contracts involving the firms that will undertake all the tasks.

Does this proposition make business sense? Probably not, because one is up against a product usually heavily subsidized by the government. But the construct of such a virtual entity (or partially reaggregated entity if you decide to undertake certain core competence tasks yourself) is becoming increasingly plausible, where it wasn't possible a few years ago.

Let's Create the Best Degree in the World!

Let's assume that the purpose of university-level education is solely to make the student as smart, skilled, and competent as possible in their chosen field—in this case, to be a great AI engineer. We'll ignore all the other objectives of a university, like learning how to think or socialization with peers.

The challenge for me, as a prospective student of AI, is that the best lecturer in the world in Course A of AI might be sitting in San Francisco, the best lecturer of Course B might be sitting in Shanghai, and the best lecturer of Course C might be sitting in Stockholm. We can probably agree that the learning (and love for a subject) one gets from a great teacher is countless times better than that of the average teacher. Specialization with the best in the field leads to immensely better outcomes.

Once we relax the frankly ridiculous TxC constraint that a student only gets credit for courses he or she completes in the college where he or she is enrolled, then the world of universities is turned on its head. Students will no longer be trapped by geography.

If I, as a student, can put together the building blocks of my own degree from the smorgasbord of excellent courses on offer around the world, that starts to be a wonderful learning proposition. If some bright entrepreneur makes this possible and accesses an on-demand degree-granting service from a prestigious university, suddenly we have a world-class offering.

Again, this university might only exist as a virtualized software platform in the cloud. No physical operations are needed. We go down through the long list of TxCs facing students (and lecturers) and eliminate them one by one.

Let's take it one step further. Is a degree-granting task actually required? For the foreseeable future, yes; the point of a degree is *trust*. It is a badge that connotes an achieved competency level that prospective employers can rely on. As we learned earlier, there are many ways of injecting trust in a situation. The astoundingly expensive medium of using a degree granted by a university may not always the best way to do so.

Over time maybe the swarm of students can meet the swarm of employers and cut out the middleman—my newly established virtualized university! Employers might potentially build trust in a student's capabilities by examining the core courses that he or she has completed, at the highest standard in the world with great lecturers, without the need for the trust-validating degree certificate. Maybe a course evaluation company will emerge that says, if our eponymous student has completed Subject A assessed by lecturer X and achieved 90 percent, then the employer can trust that the student is skilled. Or maybe, employers will be able to search across the minute detail of students' records to find graduates with the pinpoint perfect skill set to meet their needs.

TRULY PERSONALIZED EDUCATION AND MAKING EDUCATION A FLATTER, FAIRER WORLD

Given that courses (like disaggregated tasks) should be able to snap together like a child's building blocks across universities (or even non-university providers), eventually students should be able to design their own education path and have it validated in a manner that signals trust to employees and other interested parties. Fascinating multi-major combinations could be put together—neuroscience and statistics, business and genetics, marketing and computer science, mindfulness and physics.

Some might believe that remaking university-level education in such a way devalues the quality of the experience. That might be the case for that small percentage of students lucky enough (and wealthy enough) to get to attend top-of-the-pyramid brand-name universities. For most, it could augment the value of their learning experience.

For learners who face poor learning alternatives, a swarm-based, university-level offering could be spread around the world. The bright student in sub-Saharan Africa with a burning passion for bridge building can receive a first-world education that is completely validated and worthy of trust by employers and other institutions. How about delivering an MIT/Stanford/Oxford–level learning experience for high-achieving 18-year-old students in Nepal, Indonesia, and Senegal, on an almost zero marginal cost basis?

STARTING CLOSER TO HOME WITH AN EXISTING UNIVERSITY

What can the traditional university do to take advantage of falling TxCs, or even just to protect itself during this time?

A great place to start would be to generate a clear view of the landscape of tasks that the university currently undertakes—all the courses offered, the lecturers on the roster, the major blocks of research going on, the physical assets available, etc.

Then identify the TxCs that keep the university aggregated in its existing incarnation. For example, these might include rigid faculty structures that make cross-faculty education difficult.

With this inventory of tasks and clarity regarding TxCs, the university could develop alternative long-term visions that would have it taking advantage of the forces of specialization and disaggregation. Finally, the university could start with a blank sheet of paper and construct the set of tasks required to deliver the different visions it has developed. Similar to what was done for the disaggregated mortgage business in a previous chapter, it would identify the small number of tasks the university would aim to deliver at a world-class level. The universities that prepare early for a disaggregated, specialized world will be best placed.

Let's not underestimate the change management challenge that such a process would kick up. There is a good reason that most entrepreneurial opportunities are captured by small, nimble companies rather than existing institutions.

o o o

In summary, the ability to break a business down conceptually into its building block tasks gives the entrepreneur the ability to design new business propositions that might not have previously been possible.

CHAPTER 20

How Governments Can Create Value in Society Without Spending Money

All governments want to grow value within their societies and boost the happiness of their citizens. This is normally articulated through goals such as to grow incomes, to develop a business-friendly environment, to boost GDP per capita, to promote entrepreneurship and innovation.

Policy-makers rarely consider the mechanism through which value is created. With an ill-informed perspective on how value is created in society, government policy often ends up pursuing well-intentioned initiatives that diffuse efforts while investing in infrastructure for which the private sector is unwilling to pay. It is attempted value creation through subsidization of activities that are perceived as being good for business.

Scarce government resources (and, more importantly, scarce policy-making attention) should be aimed squarely at unblocking the barriers to exchange. Governments can do this by lowering transaction costs and letting the energy and entrepreneurship of the people work its magic from that point. How governments could ease the barriers to exchange could absorb all the pages of a different book, but there are some obvious lines of attack, many of which require no (or very low) direct investment of public money.

201

OPENING GOVERNMENT ASSETS TO THE ON-DEMAND ECONOMY

Governments own vast quantities of assets that are locked up and underutilized. This includes parks, woods, roads, buildings, train tracks, docks, air space, thousands of square miles of sea space, public housing, courts, hospitals, stranded pieces of land, radio spectrum, planning permissions, and the time of public servants.

According to some estimates,* the typical government assets in a developed economy amount to 200 percent or more of annual GDP, and these are "hard" assets rather than those that might be included in a much more expansive definition of assets, which may amount to 300 to 400 percent of GDP. It is hard to argue that these assets should not be deployed in the manner that best generates value and happiness for the people.

Most discussion of the usage of these assets gets tied up in a debate regarding the merits and demerits of the privatization of government assets. Putting aside privatization, perhaps idle assets should be used to earn revenues for the government in a sharing economy. Why not use an otherwise idle piece of government land for car parking if there is demand for parking in the area? Why not open most or all of government lands to hikers and walkers? While it is impossible to know what entrepreneurs might do with these assets, the liberation of these assets into the sharing economy and other exchange possibilities could release waves of new forms of exchange, boosting value in terms of entrepreneurship, employment, happiness, and tax revenue.

Clearly there needs to be close oversight to ensure that these assets are only put to good purposes. Perhaps governments might start by simply providing information as to the usage of the assets. What is their state? When have they been in use? When are they going to be in use or idle? This Internet of Things basic information is a good place to start. From there, entrepreneurs might come up with innovative proposals for how to use the assets more productively while benefiting the citizenry.

---

* IMF, *A Global Picture of Public Wealth*, 2019.

SEPARATING OWNERSHIP OF GOVERNMENT ASSETS FROM THEIR MANAGEMENT

Governments should separate the ownership of their assets from the management of those assets. Too often, the government-assigned managers of the assets (maybe a government-owned enterprise or government department) consider the assets to be "their" assets with their existing usage getting priority over all other possibly higher value users. This means assets can be stranded for decades in low-value or no-value uses.

At a simplistic level, if the assets are 200 to 400 percent of GDP and the government could earn 3 percent as a return on the assets, the government might expect to earn 6 to 12 percent of GDP annually from its assets. This might be too ambitious, but a tough mentality is required to generate value on behalf of the people, even if that value is in the simple form of the happiness of hikers enjoying walks in previously restricted areas.

For example, the typical state-owned company that manages the docks for moving goods in and out of the region might consider itself to be the owner of those docks and only use the docks for its own narrow purposes. This then inhibits the use of the assets for alternative purposes such as recreation, housing, or industrial development. Maybe the current use of those docks for moving goods into and out of a country is a low-value use of an incredible, well-located asset, close to the center of the city. Maybe the function of moving goods into and out of the country could be moved to a better location. A segregated body that "owns" all the government's assets and opens them up to their best uses (including their existing use and the sharing economy) would be in the best position to evaluate these trade-offs.

EASING TRADE BARRIERS

Trade is good, and the principles of comparative advantage still hold. But it is understandably tough for governments to relax trade barriers with other countries when there will be negative impact on specific domestic sectors that have been protected from competition from overseas firms. However, evidence shows that open trade benefits the overall population over the long run, not just with lower import prices, but also with the greater opportunities for specialization that become possible.

PROMOTING TRUST

As previously discussed, lack of trust is probably the biggest inhibitor of exchange. There are lots of ways in which governments can compensate for lack of trust. Looking at problems through a lens of trust enhancement can yield creative solutions to difficult problems that don't necessarily entail direct expenditure by the government.

Consider *pressing social issues*. In our review of trust as a TxC, we discussed the issues raised by homelessness, which could potentially be mitigated by the government (or some other body) injecting trust by acting in the role of guarantor. We must also take into account *international business relationships*. Small companies understandably find it hard to develop trade with prospective counterparties in other countries. Governments can bring trust to these situations by standing by the small company, with an implicit understanding that the small company will abide by good business practices and fulfil its obligations.

ENSURING THAT THE REAL COSTS OF A TRANSACTION ARE BORNE BY THE PARTIES TO THAT TRANSACTION

People are laden with things (inventory) given the comparatively low TxCs of owning things. Governments are not making people pay the true cost of their inventory piles. The external cost of disposing of things at the end of their useful life should be a TxC applied to the purchaser. Proper full charging of these costs might tip the balance away from low utilization ownership and toward rentership and sharing economy offerings.

For example, electronic goods are expensive to deal with at the end of their lives. Many end up being transported to less-regulated jurisdictions to be broken down and recycled. Today, some governments impose a disposal charge for electronic goods (paid by consumers at the time of buying the electronic good), though this charge may only be a fraction of the true cost of disposal.

SYSTEMATIC MINIMIZATION OF TRANSACTION COSTS

If the government of country A decided to target transaction costs in all their forms directly, this could lead to enhanced value through increased entrepreneurship. Entrepreneurs in country A would benefit from being early in bringing new propositions to market. The United States is one of the most entrepreneurial countries in the world as, on many fronts, it has lower transaction costs than other countries. Entrepreneurs in the United States benefit from earlier lowering of TxCs, leading to first mover advantage—they sometimes see the opportunities before entrepreneurs elsewhere.

In the meantime, there are plenty of places for governments to drive down transaction costs in ways that would help the citizenry:

- Tackle oligopolistic legal costs for putting together contracts.
- Increase competition for intermediaries charging higher fees than are appropriate (life insurance, asset management, etc.).
- Loosen regulatory barriers to new swarm business models (e.g., ride-sharing, accommodation).

○ ○ ○

Great ideas are the bedrock of great new business opportunities. In this book, I have covered how great ideas are not generally the result of creative brainstorming. Great ideas come from insight to the shifting landscape of transaction costs. Knowing the eight categories of transaction costs and how they are declining in the sectors you target will help you to spot great ideas before your peers. To end where we started: knowing how the world is about to turn on its axis and being first to execute on a business plan whose time has arrived is the best way to become a successful entrepreneur, and to add value and happiness to yourself and to society as a whole.

REFERENCES

The literature on transaction costs and, more specifically, how they relate to the shape of companies, the sharing economy, and new business models is growing rapidly. Among the materials that I found useful were the following:

- Akbar, Yusaf, and Andrea Tracogna. "The Sharing Economy and the Future of the Hotel Industry: Transaction Cost Theory and Platform Economics." *International Journal of Hospitality Management* 71, April 2018, 91–101.
- Chia-Ying Li, and Yu-Hui Fang. "The More We Get Together, the More We Can Save? A Transaction Cost Perspective." *International Journal of Information Management* 62, February 2022, 102434.
- Coase, Ronald. "The Nature of the Firm: Origin." *Journal of Law, Economics, and Organization* 4, no. 1 (Spring 1988), 3–17. Original article: R. H. Coase, "The Nature of the Firm," *Economica* 4, no. 16 (November 1937).
- Henten, Anders, and Iwona Windekilde. "Transaction Costs and the Sharing Economy." 26th European Regional Conference of the International Telecommunications Society, 2015.
- Lopez, Yoann. "The Transaction Costs Revolution and the Death of the Firm." Medium.com, April 1, 2016, https://medium.com/business-startup/the-death-of-the-firm-d4cde5a0ef28.

- Butler, Patrick, Ted W. Hall, Alistair M. Hanna, Lenny Mendonca, Byron Auguste, James Manyika, and Anupam Sahay. "A Revolution in Interaction." *McKinsey Quarterly*, February 1, 1997.
- Munger, Michael C. *Tomorrow 3.0: Transaction Costs and the Sharing Economy*. Cambridge University Press, 2018.
- Ricketts, Martin. *The Economics of Business Enterprise: An Introduction to Economic Organisation and the Theory of the Firm*, 3rd ed. United Kingdom: Edward Edgar Publishing, 2002.
- Smith, Adam. *The Wealth of Nations*. Oxford, England: Bibliomania.com Ltd, 2002.
- Williamson, Oliver E. "The Vertical Integration of Production: Market Failure Considerations." *American Economic Review* 61, no. 2 (May 1971), 112–123.
- Williamson, Oliver E. "Transaction Cost Economics: The Natural Progression." *Journal of Retailing* 86, no. 3 (September 2010), 215–226.

INDEX

209

ABOUT THE AUTHOR

For over 20 years, Dermot Berkery has been a partner in Delta Partners, one of the most active venture capital firms in Europe. During this time, he has evaluated over 10,000 plans for new businesses. Success in venture capital is all about understanding what is coming next rather than what is possible today. With deep experience as a venture capitalist, he has unique insights to trends in new business and, more importantly what works and doesn't work.

He worked as a consultant for McKinsey & Company in the United States and Europe and graduated from Harvard Business School. He is also the author of *Raising Venture Capital for the Serious Entrepreneur* (McGraw Hill, 2007).